ANCIENT MEMORIES, MODERN IDENTITIES

ITALIAN ROOTS IN CONTEMPORARY
CANADIAN AUTHORS

Essay Series 35

Guernica Editions Inc. acknowledges the support of The Canada Council for the Arts for its publishing program.

Canada

Guernica Editions Inc. acknowledges the financial support of the Government of Canada through the Book Publishing Industry Development Program (BPIDP) for its publishing activities.

Filippo Salvatore

Ancient Memories, Modern Identities

Italian Roots in Contemporary Canadian Authors

Translated by Domenic Cusmano

GUERNICA
TORONTO·BUFFALO·LANCASTER (U.K.)
1999

Copyright © Filippo Salvatore and Guernica Editions Inc., 1999.
Translation © Domenic Cusmano and Guernica Editions Inc., 1999.
All rights reserved. The use of any part of this publication,
reproduced, transmitted, in any form or by any means, electronic,
mechanical, photocopying, recording or otherwise stored in a
retrieval system, without the prior consent of the publisher is an
infringement of the copyright law.
Printed in Canada.
Typeset by Selina, Toronto.

Guernica Editions Inc.
P.O. Box 117, Station P, Toronto (ON), Canada M5S 2S6
2250 Military Rd., Tonawanda, N.Y. 14150-6000 U.S.A.
Gazelle, Falcon House, Queen Square, Lancaster LA1 1RN U.K.

Legal Deposit — Second Quarter
National Library of Canada
Library of Congress Catalog Card Number: 98-75366

Canadian Cataloguing in Publication Data
Salvatore, Filippo, 1948-
Ancient memories, modern identitites:
Italian roots in contemporary Canadian authors
(Essay series ; 35)
ISBN 1-55071-057-5
1. Canadian fiction (English) — Italian-Canadian authors—History
and criticism. 2. Canadian fiction (English) — 20th century —
History and criticism. 3. Identity in literature.
I. Cusmano, Domenico, 1958- II. Title.
III. Series: Essay series (Toronto, Ont.) ; 35.
PS8075.I8A53 1999 C813'.5409'851 C98-901234-4
PR9188.2.I82A53 1999

Table of Contents

Translator's Note 7

PART I: SOCIO-HISTORICAL CONTEXT OF THE ITALIAN PRESENCE IN CANADA

Origins and Historiography 13
Bruno Ramirez's *On the Move* 18
The Formation of a Little Italy in Montreal 24
The Formation of a Little Italy in Toronto:
    A Conversation with John Zucchi 28
Images of Italian Canadians:
    A Conversation with Kenneth Bagnell 34
Kenneth Bagnell's *Canadese:*
    A Portrait of the Italian Canadians 43

PART II: THE LITERATURE OF THE ITALIAN CANADIANS

The Origins of Italian Canadian Literature 53
Liborio Lattoni's *Carmina Cordis* 57
Mario Duliani's *La ville sans femmes* 64
Giose Rimanelli's *Biglietto di Terza* 74
Pietro Corsi's *La Giobba* 80
Tonino Caticchio's *La Scoperta der Canada* 84
Ermanno La Riccia's Short Stories 87
The Poets of the *Cenacolo Symposium* 91

The Voiceless People Speak Out:
    Di Cicco's *Roman Candles* 94
Antonio D'Alfonso and Guernica Editions 100
Fulvio Caccia's *Aknos* 107
C. Dino Minni's *Other Selves* 115
Marco Micone's Trilogia 120
Mary Melfi: Poetry and Prose 127
Lisa Carducci's *Héliotropes* 142
Vittorio Rossi's *Love and Other Games* 145
Nino Ricci's *Lives of the Saints* and After 152

Part III: The Cinema of the Italian Canadians

The Films of Paul Tana 163
Enigmatico: A Conversation
    with Patricia Fogliato and David Mortin 172
Notes 183

Translator's Note

This project began as a translation of Filippo Salvatore's *Tra Molise e Canada* (1994), a volume about Canadian writers of Molisan origin aimed at an Italian audience. With some minor adaptations, it was thought, the objective to familiarize Canadian readers, as well, with the work being done by a worthy but relatively unknown group of Canadian writers could be achieved.

But, as the work began, it became apparent that to limit this volume to the content of the original book would be inadequate. There were simply too many gaps to fill for a Canadian audience. Thus, the translation was enhanced by including more historical information (new chapters on Bruno Ramirez, John Zucchi and Kenneth Bagnell) as well as critiques on writers not mentioned in the original book (namely Liborio Lattoni, Mario Duliani, and Fulvio Caccia). A brief section on Italian Canadian cinema was also added to complete the survey. (It should be noted that the chapters on Caccia and Paul Tana were translated from items previously published in French, while the conversations with Kenneth Bagnell, John Zucchi, and Patricia Fogliato and David Mortin were previously published in English.) Given that almost five years had passed from the time the original (Italian) monograph was completed, the information in the existing chapters was updated.

If the Italian expression *traduttore traditore* is to be believed, then not only are translations unreliable, but the translators themselves are at best unwitting participants in the fabrication, at worst accomplices in the deception. I mention this because the expression was one often repeated by Filippo Salvatore during our travails. I'm inclined to surmise that he didn't doubt my competence as much as he was manifesting the natural apprehension that one who is fluent in the language of translation feels when he entrusts his work to a perfect stranger.

When I first met Filippo Salvatore and realized that, though slightly accented (and who doesn't speak with some accent?), his English was impeccable, my gut reaction was to ask him why he needed a translator — after all, why subject himself to such a gamble. His response was something to the effect that he needed to distance himself from his work. Well, things didn't quite work out as he expected. To say that Filippo had a hand in the translation is to understate things. This is not to imply that he meddled or that he forced my hand (except, perhaps for his insistence that the Latin expressions be kept *immutatis*). On the contrary, his interventions were welcome and they definitely improved the result — and they may even have served to alleviate his apprehension!

This said and humour aside, the final compilation, as much an adaptation as a translation, was truly a collaborative effort, and I am grateful to Filippo, not just for his suggestions but also for his openness. I also wish to thank my wife Licia Canton for her constant encouragement and for her precious comments on the early drafts of the monograph. And I want to thank my two-year-old daughter Liana for being such a great sleeper, thus allowing me to steal a couple of hours to work early mornings and late afternoons. I extend my gratitude to Multiculturalism Canada and to the Canada Council for the Arts. Finally, I would like to thank Antonio D'Alfonso for making this book possible.

Domenic Cusmano
July 1997

Part I

Socio-Historical Context
of the Italian Presence in Canada

Origins and Historiography

The Italian presence in Canada dates back to the discovery of the North American continent by the Italian explorer Giovanni Caboto in 1497 and to the exploration of its Atlantic coast by fellow Italian Giovanni da Verazzano in 1524. From the beginnings of the European colonization of the continent, this presence has remained constant, if not always sizable.

Continuity, rather than size, was indeed the focus of Father Guglielmo Vangelisti's volume on the subject entitled *Gli Italiani in Canada* (1956). The book drew attention to the important but often unacknowledged role played by the multitude of Italian nationals, mostly oversized historical figures — administrators, clergymen, soldiers of fortune — who influenced events or settled in North America over the centuries.[1] The underlying theme of Vangelisti's book is that the history of the Italian presence in Canada is both illustrious and ancient. That is, men and women of Italian origin or descent played a fundamental role in the events which shaped this country from the very start, though their Italian heritage and contribution has seldom, if ever, been recognized by the mainstream.

For instance, in *Gli Italiani in Canada* one reads that among the first settlers to arrive in New France in the seventeenth century were Italian soldiers serving France. A regiment composed mostly of Piedmontese under the command of General Carignan also settled in New France later in the seventeenth century. Equally noteworthy, according to Vangelisti, is the fact that, after the murder of LaSalle in 1687, the most powerful administrator in France's North American empire was a Neapolitan named Enrico Tonti. Elsewhere, we learn that Italian soldiers fought alongside the French in the fateful Battle of the Plains of Abraham outside Quebec City in 1759, and that during the War of 1812 the De Meuron and Watteville regiments defending Canada against the United States included numerous mercenaries of Italian origin, many of whom chose to remain in the country at the end of the hostilities. Among these were the ancestors of reputable families such as the Donegani, Burlamacchi, and Bruchesi. Vangelisti also informs his readers that during the rebellion of 1837 in Lower Canada the daughters of a certain Filippo De Grassi acted as spies for the British government forces, thus contributing to the defeat in Saint Eustache of the Patriotes led by Louis Joseph Papineau.

Gli Italiani in Canada also recounts social and political events in which Italian expatriates took part. For example, the political exile Giacomo Forneri established the first university chair in Italian language and literature in Canada when he settled in Toronto in the middle of the nineteenth century. Meanwhile in Quebec, Alessandro Gavazzi, a defrocked priest, launched a series of very heated ghibelline conferences which nearly caused him to be lynched in Quebec City by the very Catholic Irish and French Canadians faithful to the papal diktat, and which culminated in riots in Montreal where several people lost there lives.

As Vangelisti so painstakingly demonstrates, the Italian presence in Canada, particularly in Montreal, began with the earliest settlements and has endured throughout the centuries. Although Italians have been in this country from its very beginnings, a distinctive and permanent Italian entity did not begin to coalesce until the second half of the nineteenth century with the first in a series of massive migratory waves. As the relative size and importance of the Italian "colony" in Canada have increased, so too has the focus of the study of its history been shifted away from hagiography and philiopietism and more towards anthropological and sociological concerns. In the last few decades serious historical research on the subject has drawn attention to such topics as the mass immigration phenomenon and the formation of Little Italies.

This shift in focus and met hodological leap forward in the study of Italian Canadian history occurred in the 1970s thanks to the work of the late Robert F. Harney.[2] Acknowledged as the unofficial father of the new Italian Canadian historiography, Robert Harney launched Italian Canadian studies on their new course with his volume entitled *Dalla Frontiera alle Little Italies: Gli Italiani in Canada 1800-1945* (From the Border to the Little Italies) (1984). Inspired by the type of work underway in the 1960s in the United States on the various ethnic components of the American population and adopting an analytical approach akin to that of the New Left School, Harney laid the foundations for a new area of study. He enriched the study of Italian Canadian history by drawing on archival documents obtained from both Canadian and Italian sources, adding to these sociological and anthropological considerations. In addition, he focused further attention on events in the last century — a period which saw the arrival in North America of the first Italian labourers and the formation of the various Little Italies.

The epic dimension of this migration of millions of proletarians, whose exemplary contribution to their new country was met with racism and exploitation, is what Harney drew attention to in his writings and his teachings. In so doing, Harney recalls that today's urban North American professionals of Italian origin are the immediate descendants of labourers and artisans who used to make their homes in myriad tiny towns and villages throughout Italy. Whereas in the past Italian ethnicity was often repudiated, in the Canada of today it is an affirmation of identity; so much so that sociologists such as Clifford Jansen have proposed that Canadians of Italian stock no longer be marginalized as an "ethnic community," but be considered as one of the principal components of Canada's population.

By focusing attention on social phenomena such as mass immigration one can truly appreciate the heroism of the more than eight million Italians who in the course of the past one hundred years contributed to civilizing the Americas, and at the same time avoid the trap posed by hagiography and *atimìa* which Harney describes as manifestations of ethnic disesteem. Thanks to Robert Harney's thrust, the Italian presence in Canada has become a scholarly subject, and his teachings have enabled numerous students to better understand their own identity within Canadian society. Some like John Zucchi, Bruno Ramirez, Franc Sturino and Franca Iacovetta have become university professors in their own right, continuing to broaden knowledge in the field. Harney's approach, a combination of social history and anthropology, has also found an echo among several contemporary Canadian historians. Research carried out by the likes of Brown, Cook, Granatstein, Linteau, and Taschereau is evidence of this.[3] This new type of research is finally beginning to acknowledge the seminal role played by immigrants, especially Italians, in building the Canadian nation.

Bruno Ramirez's *On the Move*

French Canadian and Italian Migrants in the North American Economy: 1860 to 1914

Bruno Ramirez's book, *On the Move: French Canadian and Italian Migrants in the North American Economy: 1860 to 1914* is dedicated to the memory of Robert Harney. In the volume Ramirez establishes the links between two migratory movements which until recently have been studied separately "inserting them in a North Atlantic context of which the geographical reference points are southern Italy, Quebec and New England." He tries to understand not just the local mechanisms of the migratory phenomenon, but their international ramifications as well. Ramirez carried out primary research in local archives, in both the Molise and Campania regions of Italy, in Rhode Island, in New Hampshire, in the courthouse and the records office at Joliette, Quebec, and in the archives of the archbishopric of Montreal. By so doing Ramirez is able to paint a fairly detailed picture of the migration phenomenon and its different historical components: family, ethnic communities, agriculture, and labour. As such, he breaks down the overspecialization which characterizes contemporary historical research.

Bruno Ramirez's main goal is to "elaborate a North American perspective of the history of migrations." To do this he begins exactly where research on economic and demographic history usually stops. Contrary to the typical history of immigration, Ramirez does not limit his interest to one particular ethnic community by precisely tracing its history from the country of origin to its integration in the new society. Instead, the methodological novelty of his approach resides in the author's capacity to go beyond the geograpical and ethnic frontiers of the communities he is studying. The study of the migration of Italians and French Canadians begins from a regional perspective, but is inserted in the wider, international reality. Ramirez, in fact, highlights two main characteristics of the North American economy: the internationalization of labour and the regionalization of the markets. From this new North Atlantic perspective French Canada has been, according to Ramirez, an important geographical "switching station" for the phenomenon of migration, as a society that both received labour and exported it. One of the focal points in *On the Move* is the demonstration by means of Italian and Canadian data that the city of Montreal (the focal point of industrialization and urbanization in Canada during the period concerning the book) played a role both as a point of arrival and of sorting of labour by means of the *padrone* system to which Italian immigrants were subjected. Ramirez also analyses the reason so many Quebeckers from Berthier county migrated to New England to work in the textile mills. An essential point of reference for Ramirez in his study of the arrival and integration of the

French Canadian migrants in their new work environment is a dozen or so previous studies conducted on the industrialization of the American Northeast.

The first part of the book situates the migrants in their society of origin and explains the reasons that pushed them to migrate. The small farms owned by French Canadian settlers could barely provide enough food for subsistence. That is why droves of often very large-sized families chose to move to New England. "If our population continues to abandon this land," *La Gazette* de Berthier reported in desperation in the spring of 1892, "in a few more years, the French Canadian nation will be relocated in the United States." A parallel is drawn between conditions in Quebec and those in economically underdeveloped regions of southern Italy like Molise and the mountainous part of the province of Caserta, the *Terra di Lavoro*. After the unification of Italy in 1860, the agricultural gentry, the *galantuomini,* managed to cheaply buy back or seize land which the state had confiscated from the church and distributed to the poor peasantry. The *latifundia* system was thus strengthened and resulted in the landed gentry treating the vast majority of peasants like slaves. For the landless peasants emigrating meant acquiring their dignity as human beings. This became evident when they managed to buy a small plot of land in Italy after many hardships in the New World. As long as the peasants stayed in North America for a few years and then returned to their village of origin, Italian society received many economic benefits from the migration phenomenon. The landless peasants were willing to pay even double the price of a tract of land to free themselves of the arrogance of the *galantuomini*. Ramirez points out that the *ritornati*, although tilling the land they bought with love, end up forming "a proletariat of small proprietors." When immigration becomes permanent, it also has deleterious consequences for the village economy because the flow of money from America, which had acquired vital importance in the dynamics in the local and regional economy, ceases.

Ramirez next discusses the "migration and regionalization of the labour markets" and takes Quebec as a case study. His aim is to fill what he perceives as a lacuna in both social and labour history. He underlines the very close link which exists between the "migration phenomenon and the development of labour markets." He is convinced that a good understanding of the migration phenomenon implies demonstrating the links among migrations, labour history, economics, and demographics. According to Ramirez emigration brought about the birth of industrial capitalism. He shows the parallel growth between the several "Little Canadas" in New England and Little Italy in Montreal.

The author arrives at the following conclusion: between the beginning of the twentieth century and the World War I, "the formation of large markets, the circulation of capital resources, and the link among several regional economies produce a new social geography." The great migrations between the two shores of the Atlantic have been brought about by the needs and development engendered by American capital. Ramirez's comparative approach allows him to state that the rapport between class dynamics and migration have played a much more significant role in the south-central regions of Italy than in rural Quebec because class differences and land ownership were much more pronounced in, for example, a region like Molise. In other words, the Italian landed gentry exploited the *cafone*, or landless peasant, much more effectively. In the county of Berthier the possibility of living off the land granted to the settlers as a result of the policy of *emplacement* was greater, and there was still plenty of virgin territory left to colonize in the Quebec hinterland. The migration of rural families, therefore, ceased as soon as industrialization was managed more effectively and rapid economic growth was underway in several regions. The Quebec peasants and their many children thus found work at home and stopped emigrating to New England. Nevertheless, from the data provided by Ramirez, it is quite clear that Quebec from 1860 to the World War I played a role both as an exporter and importer of labour. The traditional image of North American historiography which portrays nineteenth-century Quebec as a static society is challenged.

However, some doubts linger as to whether Quebec's role in the growth of the North Atlantic economy was as important as Ramirez argues. After all, the total industrial labour force of the province was only 33 000 units in 1888, a tiny percentage, in real numbers, which brought about the industrial revolution in New England. One is left with the distinct impression that the thesis Ramirez presents is based upon data obtained from a single county in Quebec applied to the entire French Canadian population. The results is that this volume engages the reader as an interesting example of a comparative historical methodology, but leaves him somewhat dissatisfied with the questionable statistical results. Nonetheless, Ramirez's contribution is significant for he allows us to comprehend at the international level the very complex phenomenon of migratory movements which, because of their epic dimensions, deserve to be studied more closely than has been done until now.

The Formation of a Little Italy in Montreal

Thanks in part to the federal policy of multiculturalism, to the emergence of professors of "ethnic" origin, to the language debate in Quebec (which for obvious reasons has had to take into account the role played by allophones, particularly those of Italian origin in the protection of Quebec's French identity), the study of the Italian presence in Montreal has grown increasingly systematic and focused. It is clear, therefore, that any serious social analysis of North America's only French metropolis from the end of the nineteenth century to the present day cannot be carried out without due acknowledgment of the historical role of the immigrant communities, in particular that of the Italian community, the largest among these. According to the 1991 census figures, Greater Montreal counts some 174 000 people of single Italian heritage and an additional 42 000 of mixed Italian origin, which brings the figure of Montrealers who count at least one parent of Italian origin to well over 200 000. That is, approximately one Montrealer in ten is of Italian background.

Pays et patries: Mariages et lieux d'origine des Italiens de Montréal 1906-1930 (1987) by Sylvie Taschereau, describes some of the social practices among Montreal's early Italian immigrants. By looking at church records, her study reveals a high rate of endogamy and urban concentration among these first Italian Canadians. The cradle of the Italian "colony" in the city was St. Timothée Street which in 1875 housed several families all of whom came from the same village — Ripabottoni in the central Italian region of Molise. By 1885 Montreal counted approximately 2000 residents of Italian origin, and by 1900 the figure rose to more than 5000. By this time the Catholic religious authorities agreed that the size of the community warranted the creation of an Italian national parish. As a result, in November 1905 Jean Bruchési, archbishop of Montreal, signed the decree and in January 1906, a building located on the corner of St. Timothée and St. André Streets was acquired. The building was restored as a church and consecrated in 1907 as Madonna del Carmine. Meanwhile, some two hundred Italian families had moved further north beyond the Canadian Pacific Railway tracks to the suburban Mile-End district, occupying homes on streets such as Esplanade, St. Urbain, Clark, Grand, Beaumont, St. Dominique, and St. Laurent. Not having a parish of their own, the Italians of the Mile-End district requested and were granted permission to place their statue of the Virgin in St-Jean-de-la-Croix Church which had been erected at the corner of St. Zotique and St. Laurent Streets in 1901.

In 1910 a second Italian parish, Madonna della Difesa, was consecrated to tend to the spirituals needs of these suburban Italian residents and as a reply to the attempts made by Protestants to convert the Italians to their religion. Madonna della Difesa Church, designed in the Greek cross style, was completed in 1919 in the heart of what was to become Little Italy and hailed by Giuseppe Prezzolini, a prominent Italian intellectual who visited Montreal a few years later, as one of the most elegant churches built by Italians in North America. The project's architect was Guido Nincheri, also a renowned painter. He completed as well, over the course of two decades, the frescoes that decorate the interior of the church. The most notorious of these is a painting in the apse depicting Fascist dictator Benito Mussolini on horseback as the symbol of civilian authority. Historical research has revealed that Fascist ideology had a profound impact on Italian immigrant communities in the 1920s and 1930s through the meddling of Italian consular authorities with the support of the parish priests.[4] Fascist propaganda in Canada reached its zenith from 1929 to 1936, that is, from the *Concordato* (the pact between the Mussolini regime and the Catholic Church) to the Italian conquest of Ethiopia. Two extensive fundraising drives were undertaken during this period. Local *prominenti* with the direct involvement of the Italian consul raised money to erect a statue to Giovanni Caboto and to build a community center which became known as the Casa d'Italia. This structure, built on architect Patsy Colangelo's designs, carefully emulated the *neo-romaneggiante* aesthetic canons of the Fascist era. It was inaugurated in November 1936 and quickly became a very busy center of community activity. It still occupies the northwest corner of Jean-Talon and Lajeunesse streets. The statue of Caboto still stands in a park on the corner of St. Catherine and Atwater Streets.

The unfortunate events of World War II, which saw Italy at war with Canada, dealt a devastating blow to an otherwise thriving and well-entrenched Italian Canadian community. The state of war between the two countries resulted in the imprisonment of hundreds of innocent Italian Canadian civilians labeled a threat to Canadian national security. The horror of having the members of its elite interned indefinitely and without charges decimated the community.

Its organizations disabled and its members shamed for reasons they could not comprehend much less accept, the Italian community drifted aimlessly and without leaders. The new migratory wave, which began in the late 1940s and lasted until the end of the 1960s, infused the community with renewed vigour. But it would take more than an increase in numbers and much time before the community could rise above the humiliation and the psychological scars to begin flourishing anew.

The Formation of a Little Italy in Toronto

A Conversation with John Zucchi

F.S. You have just published *Italians in Toronto: Development of a National Identity: 1875-1934.* How did you develop the idea of writing a book on the history of the Italian presence in Toronto?

J.Z. The idea was born when Professor Robert Harney suggested that I do research work on Toronto's Italian parish registers. Luckily, the parish priests had done their job very well and it was simple to determine the parishioners' villages of origin. This was the starting point of my research. Afterwards, I was able to link this information with other documents that I found in Italy and in Toronto. The property tax rolls, the City of Toronto yearly residents' lists, and other documents have been very useful in reconstructing precisely the immigration chains from different Italian villages. I thus avoided speaking in generic or impressionistic terms about the migration phenomenon across the Atlantic.

F.S. One of the key goals in your book has been to determine the mechanisms that brought people together, and led to the development of what has become today the largest community of Italians outside Italy.

J.Z. It is true, but let me clarify something which is for me of crucial importance. Nowadays everybody speaks about an "Italian" community. From a historical point of view the matter is not so simple. During my research I was struck by the sense of belonging to a specific village or a region expressed by most of the newly arrived immigrants to Toronto, rather than to an abstract "Italian" ideal. This *campanilismo,* or feeling of belonging to a village or *paese,* manifested itself clearly in the very high rate of endogamy, that is, marriages among people from the same village, even in the second generation.

F.S. How do you explain historically and sociologically this very strong feeling of belonging to a village?

J.Z. First of all, one has to consider the so-called human chains; often times entire groups of people from the same village moved together. Each village has had its "pioneers." Toronto was one of the places where many looked for work and where they decided to stay. At the beginning, and I'm speaking about the period stretching from the middle to the end of the last century, groups of seasonal workers coming from different regions of Italy would look for work in well-defined areas. The organ grinders and musicians came from Laurenzana, in the province of Potenza; the fruit vendors came from Termini Imerese in the province of Palermo in Sicily. (In the first decades of the century almost a quarter of all Toronto fruit vendors were Sicilians.) The *mosaicisti* and *terrazzieri* (mosaic and tile setters) came from Friuli, especially from

Fanna, and knife-grinders came from Val Rendena in the province of Trento. The *campanilismo* can thus be explained in different ways. The migrants' origins, from only a handful of towns, has allowed them to recreate within Toronto, several mini-villages. Moreover, the hostility of the surroundings obliged the immigrants to maintain, out of necessity, a strong attachment to their village of origin and to their own traditions.

F.S. This *campanilismo* can easily be explained from an Italian perspective. Nonetheless, from an English Canadian point of view, the new immigrants were simply "Italians." How did the move from a village identity to an Italian identity take place?

J.Z. Let us not forget that every immigrant from whichever region of Italy he came had a superficial sense of being Italian. Inevitably, in his daily life and in his working relations, a Sicilian or a Friulian, notwithstanding their many differences, had Italy as their common reference point. In my work I insisted upon isolation and on the birth of a ghetto mentality without any derogatory connotation. To begin with, the migrants' isolation was physical. Residential segregation, as a consequence of the industrialization of the city, relegated the budding Italian "colony" to three districts: The Ward, College and Grace Streets, and Dufferin and Davenport Streets. Religion was a second cause of isolation. The Irish Catholic hierarchy treated Italians as a specific ethnic group: the "Italians" were viewed as one of the components of an essentially Irish dioceses. A result of this attitude had been management of the Italian problem by Irish priests or religious orders.

Slowly but surely, the consciousness arose that Italians did constitute a specific homogeneous group. The third factor which enabled the birth and the development of an Italian identity was the behaviour and the rhetoric of the community leaders, the so-called *prominenti*. The few professionals, the *padroni* or job providers, the bankers, the shopkeepers, the "ethnic canvassers" for the various political parties, the most politicized elements within the colony that kept up even in Canada with the political situation in the mother country: all of these people in a different manner or for different reasons favoured the emergence a trans-village or trans-regional, and therefore "Italian," identity.

F.S. Various groups of Italian origin have been present in Toronto since the second half of the last century. However, when did a colony in the true sense, that is, with a structure and its specific identity, emerge?

J.Z. The English-language press began to use the concept since the last decade of the last century. A little permanent colony existed then in Toronto, but most of its members consisted of seasonal workers who often ended up returning to Italy. It is with the outbreak of World War I that a true Italian identification manifests itself. Toronto Italians had the feeling of belonging, and were proud of this belonging, to a specific ethnic group. The fact that Canada and Italy were allies, no doubt, favoured the emergence of this awareness.

F.S. Your volume covers also the 1920s and 1930s. How did the Italian colony in Toronto and the English-language Canadian press react to the birth of the Fascist movement and to Mussolini's rise to power?

J.Z. Since the very beginning, the reaction was positive and a pro-Fascist attitude prevailed in Toronto. The official English-language media saw Mussolini as a bulwark against communism and supported him. The majority of the community became familiar with the political situation in Italy and adhered to the Fascist regime thanks to overwhelming propaganda spread by the Italian consuls and vice-consuls and the Catholic parish priests and Protestant pastors who knowingly confused love for one's origins with Fascism. The Italian colony's behaviour was not very different from the attitude expressed by other Canadians towards charismatic leaders from the right such as Aberhart, the founder of Social Credit in Alberta, or Maurice Duplessis in Quebec. It is important to remember that both English and French Canadian public opinion felt sympathy towards Mussolini up to 1935, the date of the Ethiopian crisis. It is precisely to underline the change of perception of the Fascist regime in English Canada that I chose the year 1935 as the cut-off date in my work. The cult of the strong personality can be viewed as a consequence of a desperate search for solutions to the grave economic crisis with which the democratic regimes could not cope in the 1930s.

F.S. What ought to be the future direction of historical research on the Italian presence in Canada?

J.Z. In the 1970s and 1980s the Italian presence in Canada up to the 1930s especially in Quebec and Ontario has been the main field of research. Grave lacunae remain, nonetheless, both for the Maritime Provinces and the Canadian West. We are still lacking an up-to-date synthesis of the national history of Canadians of Italian origin. A number of young scholars are studying the period of the World War II, and the results should be out soon. We need to analyze, using scientific criteria, the Italian presence in Canada from the 1940s to the present. It is a phenomenon that constitutes a very wide field of research because of its epic dimension. A growing number of young researchers will, no doubt, obtain many worthwhile results in the years to come.

Images of Italian Canadians

A Conversation with Kenneth Bagnell

F.S. In the preface to *Canadese: A Portrait of the Italian Canadians* (1989), you write that your book should be considered the work of a journalist rather than a scholarly product.[5] Explain, first of all, why. Clarify, moreover, why you acknowledge your debt and gratitude to the historian Robert Harney. What do you owe him exactly?

K.B. I feel an enormous gratitude towards Robert Harney. It was he who suggested to me, in various meetings, the direction and the nuances crucial to the correct understanding of the complex nature of the Italian Canadian identity and community structures. I believe his emphasis kept me from going astray and from being hammer-handed. Many times he would say about italophobia and the criminal stereotype: "It is all a matter of context." I owe him that. As to my method, I have this to clarify. The methodological approach in *Canadese* is the same as the one I used in my work as a journalist. I followed the structure of a novel but all facts are true. You will see this, to give an example, in the description of the internment camps. I spent an enormous amount of time to get the small details of what the Italian Canadian "enemy aliens" ate and did to pass the time in the camp at Petawawa. These details allowed me to better understand the emotional dimension of their life and, as a result, construct the narrative of the chapter along the novelistic line. So, my methodology, and by that I mean the structure and prose style are drawn from my past and are already reflected in my previous book *Little Immigrants*. Professor Harney's contribution to my understanding the mentality of Italian Canadians is very great. I truly regret he did not live to see my work in print. His premature death is a loss to scholarship, but also a personal loss.

F.S. Why did you decide to leave out of your treatment the Italian presence in Canada before the beginning of the twentieth century?

K.B. I acknowledge in my book that there had been an Italian presence in Canada before the first big wave of immigration towards the beginning of this century. But I chose that date as a dividing line for several reasons. Let me say that *Canadese* is a portrait, not a history of the Italian Canadians in the twentieth century. Why did I start then? Because one of the landmarks of the Italian experience in Canada was the Cordasco episode, which opened the century. That is, the inquiry by Judge John Winchester into the activity of private entrepreneurs or *padroni*. His report to the federal government led to the Alien Labour Bill which sharply disciplined the recruiting of labourers by the railway and steamship companies through private agencies. In the Cordasco episode I was keen to show how the dominant British Canadian culture exploited the Italian navvy. Cordasco was an opportunist who profited because he fitted in the prevalent attitude of the time. He was simply the servant of John Burns, the Canadian Pacific Railway hiring agent. There is also a second reason for choosing the beginning of the century as a starting date. A Royal Commission was called, and its documentation was available, which enabled me to do descriptive narrative, fundamental to my work and interest. Some of the young scholars who read the book, I am pleased to say, understand what my intent was. I am grateful I have the respect of scholars, even though they know, as I know, I am not doing scholarship. But I must have been doing something valid if they recognize the validity of my work.

F.S. One of the striking elements in your book is the close link you establish between the Italian minority and the prevailing national Canadian issues of the time. It must have been one of your main concerns and that is why, I suppose, you deal with the issue of the behaviour of the Royal Canadian Mounted Police so sternly. The formation of a Fifth Column and the acts of sabotage the "enemy aliens" were about to commit were, in truth, and you show it very well, a trumped up charge. This is especially true in the case of industrialist James Franceschini, who was arrested right after he had offered to help the Canadian government build frigates at the outbreak World War II.

K.B. No doubt. As a child in a tiny Nova Scotia town in June 1940 seeing Italian men being taken away by the police, it left a permanent memory on my life which is still engraved and comes back. The internment was, for the Italian Canadians, a historic tragedy. Because of the iniquitous decision taken by Ottawa, a lot of harm was visited upon the Italians and they did not recover from it for two decades. While they were on the verge of finding a place in Canada and a sense of pride, they were decimated, their leaders interned, their press silenced, their organizations destroyed. As a result of the War Measures Act of 1940 the Italians in Canada became leaderless, rejected and dejected. Why did they receive such a harsh treatment? It was a combination of things. It was brought about by hysteria, italophobia, and ignorance. I believe it reflected the prevalent notion of the time — the 1930s and 1940s. Italians who came from a land of rich culture were regarded as something less than fully human, literally beasts of burden. The historic wrong they suffered remains a blot on Canadian history.

F.S. Would you, therefore, agree that the Canadian government owes an apology to the Italian Canadians? Should the government officially acknowledge its wrong as it did recently in the case of Japanese Canadians?

K.B. Yes, it should. As I travel across the country to promote *Canadese* I am asked the same question everywhere, often by interviewers who know nothing about internments and are shocked by them. I have met the leaders of the National Congress of Italian Canadians and at their request I am acting as a resource person to strengthen their case and urge the federal government to apologize. I am doing so not on the basis of emotion or sentimentality but on the facts I have uncovered. It is plainly a matter of justice. The internments were not warranted, as G. Robertson, the leading civil servant of the day in charge of security matters, said in his report to Justice

Minister Ernest Lapointe. He noticed that even the members of the *fasci* were not at heart disloyal. Being a *fascio* member was quite acceptable in Canada, especially in Quebec. Moreover, the Italians who had joined the Fascist organizations did so out of loyalty to the homeland they had left, out of sentimental feeling. L. Frenza, a shoemaker from Montreal was typical. He told me he had joined the *fascio* just as he had joined every other organization. He admitted that joining the *fascio* was a strategic error and unwise, but he was not, never had been, and would never be but a law-abiding citizen. His loyalty to Canada was indisputable. All men I interviewed in the early 1980s are dead or about to die. We, as Canadians, owe them and their families who suffered the ignominy of unjust internment, an apology.

F.S. Is there a special reason why the first part of your book ends with the World War II and the second part begins with the second wave of immigration?

K.B. Yes, there is. In the same way as there are two ages of Canada — pre-war and post-war — similarly there have been two ages of Italian immigration. Hence, it seemed natural to begin the second part of *Canadese* with the new wave of immigration. The people who came after 1945 came from a new social reality were of a different mental outlook and did different things once they arrived in Toronto, Montreal, or Vancouver. The previous generation had, because of the internment, a very injured psychological make-up. The newcomers did not.

F.S. Both, at the beginning of the century in the twin cities of Fort William and Port Arthur, and especially in the late 1950s and early 1960s in Toronto and Southern Ontario, Italian labourers and construction workers were involved in labour disputes. Why did you attach a lot of importance to the role they played in bringing about the birth of unions in English Canada?

K.B. I devoted two chapters to the involvement of Italian Canadians in the birth and rise of the union movement in Canadian labour history simply because as a reporter my task was to write about Italians where they were early on and up to the early 1960s. As the 1961 census showed, they were still essentially labourers and to an extent they still are. It was natural for me to write about Italians and the formation of unions because that was the only way to be historically accurate. Why did I pick the Deprenzo brothers' wounding and the Hogg's Hollow cave-in as the two examples? Because they made vivid the mistreatment given to Italians. In the case of the Deprenzo brothers independent witnesses said they were shot at by the police when they themselves were unarmed and not engaged in physical violence of any kind. In fact, one police officer, after one of the Deprenzo brothers had been wounded, actually picked him up so that one of his colleagues could fire at him again. The irony is that they, who were the target of violence, went to prison for ten years, whereas no policeman was ever charged. As for the Hogg's Hollow incident, it reveals a number of truths: how lacking safety measures were in Ontario at that time. Toronto and the rest of the province were embarked in a tremendous construction boom, but thought very little or not at all of the men doing the dirty work. They descended into tunnels without any training, without hard hats or work boots or even flash lights. The safety measures of the early 1960s for the immigrant labourers were the same as those of the 1880s.

F.S. So the reason your book is dedicated to the memory of the five construction workers who met death together in the prime of their life on the evening of March 17, 1960, in Toronto because of the cave-in of the tunnel in which they were working . . .

K.B. . . . Is a very obvious one. *Canadese* is a book about everyday Italians on everyday streets in Canada. My dedication to their memory is an indication of my feelings towards their atrocious death and a token of my appreciation.

F.S. In your book you deal with the career of Judge Angelo Branca from Vancouver and the conflicts that emerged among British Columbia Italians when the cultural center was built. You also speak, in another chapter, about the manner in which the Italian community in Quebec became the target of resentment by French Canadian nationalists during the Saint-Leonard language crisis in the late 1960s and the emergence of a new leadership in the mid 1970s with people like Pietro Rizzuto in Montreal and Pietro Bosa in Toronto. Proportionally, however, the lion's share of the content belongs to Ontario and to Toronto. *Canadese* can be accused of being Toronto-centric. There are Italian communities in all the Canadian provinces, yet the Maritimes and the Prairies, for instance, do not appear at all in the book. Is this not a weakness of your volume that aspires to be a portrait of all Italian Canadians from coast to coast?

K.B. That is a fair criticism. But let me explain why I wrote the book the way I did. First of all, the population of Italians in Southern Ontario is by rough but reliable estimate half a million strong and many crucial elements took place among them. Since I live among them and travel in that area, it may be that I gave more weight to them than they deserve. But, given the size of the population, that criticism is a matter of opinion. I told the people in the Prairies that it is my intention to give them much more attention in the second book I plan to write. This will be an oral history of the communities in Winnipeg, Edmonton and British Columbia. I will start working on it in the coming months.

F.S. In the last two chapters of the book, "Put It in Writing: Italian Canadians Look Inward" and "Home Is Where the Heart Is", you touch on a crucial question: that of identity and belonging. You rightly mention that young writers are looking inward and expressing the trauma and the lingering existential ambivalence between the old and the new world, between the peasant traditions of Southern Italy and the urban, post-industrial reality of cities like Montreal and Toronto. You also point out that Italian Canadians now are more accepted by English and French charter groups. Nonetheless, the criminal stigma still remains an obstacle to full partnership in mainstream Canada. Generally speaking, Italian Canadians are nowadays quite well off, but there is a growing spiritual vacuum felt by both the old generation which finds it difficult to cope with the new social role it is called upon to play, and especially the second and third Canadian-born generations. That is, too many young people of potential simply settle for the easy dollar and seem to forget that there is more to being a rich person than just material goods. There is culture and spiritual depth. Do you not think this is a debate that goes beyond the Italian Canadian ethnic group and is, instead, an integral part of the issue about the nature of Canadian identity *tout court,* and an essential element of the debate on how to cope ethically with a materialistic and consumer-oriented world view?

K.B. I do. I believe that more than any other immigrant group the Italian communities still retain a spiritual dimension, and while they suffer the same erosion of a materialistic and hedonistic age, they have more opportunity to feel the vacuum and fill it through the help of social workers and the support of the family. The solutions Italian Canadians will find to cope with their own search for identity to overcome the lure of consumerism and materialism will help shape our national identity and destiny. The Italians will contribute to it, perhaps, more than any other group in our society.[7]

Kenneth Bagnell's *Canadese*

A Portrait of the Italian Canadians

Canadese: A Portrait of the Italian Canadians by Kenneth Bagnell is one of the finest books so far on the Italian presence in Canada. Unlike the type of research usually carried out by professional historians, this — as the author himself acknowledges — is a book written by a journalist which draws in large part on the everyday life of everyday people. As such, the author's target audience is not the specialist, but anyone in the public at large who has an interest in the history and the identity of Canada's fourth largest ethnic component — the Italians — which according to the 1991 census officially number approximately one million people.

One need only compare *The Italians in Canada* by Antonino Spada which appeared in Montreal in 1969 to Bagnell's book to appreciate just how far the study of Italian issues in Canada has come. Spada was content to merely paraphrase, for an English-speaking audience, much of the information contained in *Gli Italiani del Canada* by Vangelisti,[9] thereby sketching a rough portrait of the Italian presence, particularly in Quebec, from the discoveries of the New World to the first few decades of the twentieth century. He only hinted, for instance, at how Fascism in Italy affected the lives of Italians living in Canada; that hundreds of Italian Canadians were imprisoned in 1940 by the Canadian government for nothing more than being perceived as a threat to national security. Similarly, Spada merely alluded to the existence of Italian communities elsewhere in Canada with the mention of superficial and often inaccurate information.

In contrast, the portrait of the Italian Canadians painted by Kenneth Bagnell adopts an interpretive perspective which owes much — and Bagnell acknowledges this in his preface — to Robert Harney. Like Harney, Bagnell has chosen to explore the events of the first eighty years of this century. However, contrary to the professional historian, Bagnell does not limit himself to a mere analysis of the facts. Rather, he employs historical data to bring the events to life. His narrative account could be considered novelistic inasmuch as each of the twelve chapters which comprise the book contains characters who "relive" the historical events in which they took part or which they witnessed. A striking characteristic of *Canadese* is the accuracy of the historical context in which the characters evolve. In the first part of the book, Bagnell employs material obtained from archives or from daily papers; in the second part, he relies instead on people's oral accounts. Throughout, the unifying elements of the text are the immediacy of the dialogue and the incisiveness of the description. What we have here is a unique work, which, although replete with historical facts, is not characterized by the heaviness which often accompanies historical research. *Canadese* is a book which is pleasant to read in part due to its incisive but flowing style and to the dramatic nature of the events which are described.

In the first chapter we are the spectators during Justice John Winchester's inquiry which sought to expose and, thereby, eliminate the mechanisms of exploitation characterized by *padronismo,* a system for hiring and exploiting navvies, of which Antonio Cordasco, in cahoots with Canadian and British railway and shipping companies, was a leading exponent. We thus become acquainted with a savage form of capitalism which allowed poor Southern Italian farmers to enter the country, only to be exploited as labourers.

The second chapter describes the overtly brutal contempt and racism with which the Italian immigrants, "a throng of ignorant and stinking bastards, braggarts and mere nut vendors" were regarded. Italian workers were perceived as nothing more than beasts of burden, and that was the way they were treated. Exploitation and mistreatment of Italian immigrant workers in the towns of Fort William and Port Arthur (present-day Thunder Bay) came to a head with strikes marked by brawls and other forms of violence. In one incident two brothers, Domenico and Nicola Deprenzo, are assaulted and wounded by police gunfire and then condemned to ten years in prison. Labeling its own residents agitators and undesirables was the method which Canadian society used to protect itself against perceived threats.

Bagnell next describes the insufferable living conditions of the tiny Italian community in Toronto's Ward district, the prejudice of the English-language press, and the life of James Franceschini. Originally from Aquila, a city in the Abruzzo region of Italy, Franceschini came to Canada to work as a construction worker's helper; but in a short while, owing to his hard work and his spirit of entrepreneurship, he set up his own business digging foundations. In just a few years he had become a major contractor in the construction of roads and highways. But the honest Ontario resident was labeled a threat to national security, arrested by the RCMP and interned as an "enemy alien" following Mussolini's declaration of war on the Allies in 1940. The same iniquitous fate befell hundreds of other innocent people — the elite of the various Italian communities in cities throughout the country — labeled Fascist sympathizers ready to transform themselves into a Fifth Column of hostile and subversive infiltrators and agitators. As a result of hysteria, intolerance, racism, and latent italophobia, the Canadian government proclaimed the War Measures Act giving itself the power to indefinitely detain any suspect without laying any charges. The outcome of these measures saw many innocent people, who could never even imagine betraying their adopted land, interned in concentration camps in Fredericton and Petawawa, some for as long as four years.

Bagnell labels this incident an ignominious act which left Italian Canadians humiliated and very deeply scarred. It is only with the arrival of the second wave of immigrants, at the end of World War II, that the indignity visited by the Canadian government upon many of its own citizens was set aside, but not forgotten. The new Italian immigrants were characterized by a different psychological outlook, even if they, too, at first had to be satisfied with occupying the lowest rungs on the social ladder. The women set off to work in clothing factories, while the men headed for the construction sites and contributed in literally building the infrastructures which today make up the country. But their lives were often at risk since safety on construction sites was almost non-existent and incidents were numerous. The most serious occurred at Hogg's Hollow in March of 1960 when five workers who were digging a tunnel died as a result of a landslide. Only after such an appalling tragedy did the Ontario government undertake to pass measures to reduce the dangers on construction sites. Meanwhile people like John Stefanini worked hard to convince workers to join labour unions.

As the years went by, the economic and social conditions of the majority of Italian Canadians improved. But many others felt a sense of emptiness rising from within themselves. Some tried to overcome this emptiness and anxiety by moving back to their hometown in Italy. But they quickly realized that they were deluding themselves if they thought they could go back. So many years spent in Toronto or in any other Canadian city made Canadians out of them and Canada was where they belonged. The existential rift between two physical and ideological realities becomes the principal theme of a new generation of Italian-Canadian writers like Frank Paci. Like many other young authors, Paci celebrates his parents' courage and describes how, after many hardships and sacrifices, they find themselves in an enviable economic position.

What makes Bagnell's book worth reading is its ability to trace an accurate portrait of the Italian Canadian identity until the 1980s. In so doing, Bagnell describes the role of Italian Canadians in the often acrimonious linguistic debate between anglophones and francophones in the 1960s and 1970s in Quebec. He describes in detail the confrontation in St. Leonard between italophones and francophones, and the language of instruction debate which was "resolved" by the Parti Québécois government with the passage of Bill 101 in 1977, obliging everyone, except those whose mother tongue is English, to attend French school. Bagnell highlights the diverging opinions extant within the Italian Quebecois community concerning language, but also focuses attention on people like Pietro Rizzuto in Montreal, and Pietro Bosa and Lino Magagna in Toronto as the leaders in efforts to unite all Canadians of Italian origin under one banner: the National Congress of Italian Canadians. The existence of such an organization is all the more essential to counteract the effects of the stereotypical perceptions by outsiders of Italians as mobsters.

In the concluding chapter, the author of *Canadese* touches upon the aspirations and the as yet unresolved issues confronting the Italian Canadians. But the sound of his words inescapably echoes an ugly and painful truth. In the last decade or so Italian Canadians have come a long way with many occupying positions of prestige, but the aspirations of the second and third generation of Italian Canadians often seem limited to mere material gain. Many young people allow themselves to be seduced by the almighty dollar, forgetting that spiritual and cultural enrichment is an indispensable premise to their social integration and their success. Plainly, Kenneth Bagnell's book is an accurate and up-to-date source of information on the Italian presence in Canada since the turn of the century. Its scope is wide-reaching yet profound; its narrative engaging yet easy to read. *Canadese* is without a doubt an outstanding volume on the Italian Canadian identity. It will open the eyes of all those who wish to understand the true nature of our society. If the concept of multiculturalism stands for more than mere folklore and must contribute to the acceptance of diversity and equality, then *Canadese* by Kenneth Bagnell is a splendid example of the type of reading that should be proposed to the Canadian public.

Part II

The Literature of the Italian Canadians

The Origins of Italian Canadian Literature

The existence, today, of a distinctive and substantive Italian Canadian literary corpus can trace its progress alongside the development of the Italian Canadian community, which has its roots in the massive migratory movements of the late nineteenth century and the post-World War II period. As the community has grown from tiny isolated and inward-looking "encampments" to a large, widespread and resourceful entity, so too have its writers become more outspoken and more visible. Two, Fulvio Caccia and Nino Ricci, were recent recipients of the Governor General's award.

But despite the attention that Italian Canadian writing has enjoyed lately, its emergence as a bona fide and distinctive area of study has been anything but constant and its survival far from certain. Early writers were few, as members of a community of uneducated, immigrant labourers, whose mere survival was a source of constant apprehension, put little stock in breeding poets and intellectuals in large numbers. Nevertheless, a skeletal but sophisticated class of writers was present during the early years of the Italian Canadian community's existence, which in hindsight provided the foundation for the new and broader order of writers which has emerged since the

1970s. Though arbitrary, it is perhaps helpful to use the 1970s as a watershed to examine the evolution of Italian Canadian writing. Indeed, clear and distinctive features as much unite writers in the period before 1970 as they differentiate them from the writers who have come along in the late 1970s and throughout the 1980s. Early Italian Canadian writers can generally be described as male immigrants who came to Canada as adults with a relatively high level of education. They were somewhat established or already laboured in intellectual fields such as journalism or education. The topics of their writings usually revolved around the hardships of the immigrant experience seen from within, sprinkled with the occasional lyric, usually written in Italian.

Among these was educator and Protestant pastor Liborio Lattoni who, in Montreal in the period between the two world wars, wrote patriotic poetry in Italian, reminiscent of Carducci. In Toronto during the same period, Francesco Gualtieri wrote poetry in English. An anti-Fascist, Gualtieri is best remembered as the author of the first, if somewhat brief, history of Italians in Canada which appeared in 1928 entitled *We Italians*. Another writer who describes the Canadian reality from an Italian perspective is journalist A. Napolitano in his book *Troppo grano sotto la neve* (An Over Abundance of Wheat Beneath the Snow). The volume culls together a series of impressionistic observations on French Canada, particularly Montreal in the 1930s, and the Italians living in its midst. It is similar in intent to Mario Soldati's *America primo amore* (America First Love). Among the pioneers of Italian Canadian literature is also the journalist and playwright Mario Duliani, who arrived in Montreal in 1936 and who wrote mostly in French. Though Duliani's principal occupation was the theatre, he is probably best remembered for his semi-autobiographical novel *La Ville sans femmes* (The City Without Women[8]) published in 1945 about the events surrounding the arrest and internment at the beginning of World War II of the so-called "enemy aliens" (Canadians of Italian origin alleged to be Fascist sympathizers) by Canadian authorities.

The post-World War II period produced a new but somewhat similar wave of Italian Canadian writers, that is, a class of educated immigrants who, like their predecessors in the earlier part of the century, came to Canada as adults with the intention of working in intellectual domains. Among these are Giose Rimanelli, Pietro Corsi, Umberto Taccola, Gianni Grohovaz, Camillo Carli, Dino Fruchi, Tonino Caticchio, Ermanno La Riccia, Maria Ardizzi, Matilde Torres, Corrado Mastropasqua, and Romano Perticarini. Using Italian as their language of expression, these writers convey views and concerns similar to those of the previous generations, that is, the difficulty of adjusting to the New World and the alienation of deracination faced by the emigrant. Two notable examples in this vein are the often introspective yet vivid prose works of Rimanelli and Corsi. *The Italians in Canada* (1969), a historical account of the Italian presence in Canada, mentions other names active in the literary field. However, its author, Montreal former anti-Fascist activist and founder of the weekly *Il Cittadino canadese* in 1941, Antonino Spada makes it plain that until then the Italian contribution to Canadian literature was quite meager.

The Italian Canadian writers who began to make their mark beginning in the 1970s can be distinguished from their foregoing counterparts by several characteristics. That is, contrary to the earlier writers, most are the sons and daughters of first generation immigrants, born in Canada or Italy, but raised and educated in Canada. Although some publish mostly in Italian, the majority publish in English or French, sometimes in both, and at times in all three languages. The focal point of their work, like their forebears, inevitably began with the immigrant experience, but evolved to include the contrast between the southern rural heritage and the Canadian northern urban reality. A strong current also explores the search for roots, at times laced with a touch of nostalgia. In addition, while early Italian Canadian writers tended to limit their scope to their immediate community, the current crop of writers sees the public at large as its target audience. Among Italian Canadian writers of the current generation are Frank Paci, Dino Minni, Pier Giorgio Di Cicco, Alexandre Amprimoz, Joseph Pivato, Marco Micone, Antonio D'Alfonso, Fulvio Caccia, Mary di Michele, Antonino Mazza, Mary Melfi, Vittorio Rossi, Nino Ricci, Caterina Edwards, and Pasquale Verdicchio.

Liborio Lattoni's *Carmina Cordis*

Liborio Lattoni was born in 1874 in Urbisaglia, a small town in the Marches region of central Italy. He obtained a degree in literature and philosophy in Florence where he was a pupil of the renowned poet and senator Guido Mazzoni. Unable to find a satisfying occupation in his homeland, he moved to Switzerland, and in 1907 to New York, where he lived for a few months. On January 19, 1908, at the age of thirty-four he settled in Montreal at the urging of his friend Torquato Spadone. Meanwhile, he had converted to Protestantism and become a pastor of the Methodist Church. In Montreal, the Canadian city with the largest Italian "colony," Lattoni was assigned the task of running a school for the sons and daughter of Italian immigrants and directing the small Italian Protestant congregation. His unofficial duty, however, was to "Canadianize" the Italians under his responsibility by having them learn to speak English and French and, more importantly, by converting them to Protestantism.

In 1910 his wife Ada, a girl from the well-to-do Florentine bourgeoisie, joined him with their two children, Jenny and Mario. Jenny, a nice girl with a frail constitution, died of a congenital heart ailment at around the age of twenty. She was very much missed by her father who expressed his distress over her loss for many years in his poetry. Mario, a bright fellow, earned a degree in law at

Université de Montréal and practiced law for over fifty years in Montreal. He died in 1993 at the age of ninety-two. Notwithstanding a certain diffidence that the Italian community felt towards him (that is, as a result of clashes between Italian Catholics and Protestants in 1910), Liborio Lattoni managed to convert a sizable proportion of Italians to Protestantism, often by finding them work.

Because of the *Questione romana* (the pope considered himself a prisoner of the new Kingdom of Italy which had annexed Rome in 1870), Catholic priests were prevented from assuming an active political role. The Italian consular authorities preferred to have dealings with Italian Protestant pastors. Right from the start, Liborio Lattoni played a pivotal role in shaping the fortunes of Montreal's Italian community in the early part of this century.

In 1915 when Italy entered the war as an ally of both England and France, Liborio Lattoni became a fervent propagandist for the need to participate in the war, convincing scores of young Italian immigrants to enlist and go overseas to defend their homeland. In the French-speaking parts of Canada, namely Quebec, public opinion did not share English Canada's view of Italy's declaration of war. For the French Canadians it was merely a pretext for England's allies to defend their national standing and to pursue their policy of grandeur, not to fight against the German-speaking "barbarians." *Le Devoir* publisher Henri Bourassa denounced Italy's decision to enter the war, and instead defended the Vatican's view to remain neutral. Bourassa's position inflamed the passions of the Italian consul and those of the community leaders who organized a patriotic gathering at Champ de Mars, in the center of the city, to which over ten thousand people participated.

As one of the speakers Liborio Lattoni demanded the liberation of Trento and Trieste and accused the Austrians and Germans of being lawless barbarians. He also criticized Henri Bourassa. So aroused, the mob made its way to *Le Devoir* and ransacked its offices. Following accusations that he had been the instigator, Lattoni replied in a letter published in English by saying that on the contrary he had attempted to pacify the mob; the journalists had misinterpreted his remarks! All the same, after the incident Lattoni's reputation as a leading spokesman for the Italian community soared.

Lattoni took a very active role in the life and development of Montreal's Italian community for the following two decades. In 1923 it is mostly thanks to his efforts that the Grand Quebec Lodge of the Order of the Sons of Italy was founded. He also became, immediately after the March on Rome in October 1922, a convinced defender of Fascism. To him the Duce was a bulwark against the communist threat; the embodiment of the resurrected greatness of Ancient Rome and the new destiny that Italy as a great nation was called upon to play henceforth. Lattoni approved of Italy's conquest of Abyssinia in 1936. Patriotism and Fascism became in Lattoni's mind synonymous, as they did for the great majority of North American Italians.

Liborio Lattoni initiated and actively participated, during the mid 1920s, in the Campagna Caboto, an attempt to demonstrate that it had been the Venetian Giovanni Caboto, and not the Frenchman Jacques Cartier, who had discovered Canada on June 24, 1497, coincidentally St-Jean-Baptiste Day, the traditional national holiday of French Canada. Lattoni's and the Italian community's claim was resented by French-speaking public opinion, of which Henri Bourassa was a spokesman, as an attempt to undermine French Canada's historical legitimacy as one of this country's two founding nations. When in 1933 the bronze statue of Giovanni Caboto by sculptor Guido Cassini was unveiled at the corner of Atwater and Ste-Catherine Streets, the Montreal municipal council forbade that the inscription in the pedestal read: *Scopritore del Canada* (Discoverer of Canada).

In 1933 Lattoni was among the community leaders who welcomed the Italian aviation ace Italo Balbo during his stopover in Montreal after crossing the Atlantic with a squadron of twenty-four hydroplanes en route to the universal exposition in Chicago. In November 1936 the Casa d'Italia was officially inaugurated and it immediately became a very active community center. It was also a base for Fascist indoctrination and propaganda. In 1939 Liborio Lattoni with fellow-Italian expatriate, journalist and playwright Mario Duliani founded the Centro Culturale Italiano, where the Italian community's elite and French-Canadian audiences were able to appreciate authors like Luigi Pirandello and Gabrielle D'Annunzio. On June 10, 1940 when Italy declared war on France, England, and by extension Canada, the Canadian government invoked the War Measures Act. Liborio Lattoni was arrested, as were hundreds of other supposed Italian Canadian Fascist sympathizers, but was released after only a few months thanks to the intervention of the Methodist Church of Canada. He was sixty-six years of age.

The years between 1940 and 1945 were a period of great sadness and discouragement for Lattoni. The war being waged between Canada and Italy between 1940 and 1943 and the Italian civil war between 1943 and 1945 obliterated his beliefs and dampened his high-sounding rhetoric. The tragedy of war, destruction, and hunger in his country of birth turned Liborio Lattoni towards his poetry. Scores of his poems were published in the Montreal Italian-language anti-Fascist weekly *Il Cittadino canadese.*

Lattoni had been writing poems since 1915, publishing several in Italian language publications such as *Il Carroccio* and *Il Progresso italo-americano* in New York. In the early years their recurring theme was the greatness of Rome and of the new Italy. Lattoni echoed the great nineteenth century Italian poet Giosué Carducci, Nobel Prize for literature in 1904. However, in his later years until his death in 1958 at the age of eighty-four, Lattoni reverted to more lyrical themes: the passage of time usually presented at sunrise or sunset, the weight of old-age, the increasingly ethereal remembrance of Florence, the everlasting love for his country of birth, and the growing awareness expressed more and more clearly of belonging to Canada — of having become truly an Italian Canadian, a human hybrid. He articulated the seminal theme of the split identity; the notion of being suspended between two worlds characteristic of a good deal of Italian Canadian literature today.

In 1946 the pages of *Il Cittadino canadese* carried an announcement of the forthcoming publication in New York of a collection of Lattoni's poetry. The title of the volume was *Carmina Cordis* (Songs from the Heart) and would have comprised over 500 poems written since 1915. Unfortunately the volume never appeared. Searching in the archives of *Il Cittadino canadese* from 1941 to 1958 I found over forty poems, which in my opinion represent the most mature and sincere phase of Lattoni's writings.

Lattoni's poems are striking for their elegance both in form and style. From a technical point of view, his poetry is praiseworthy. He uses different metric forms with great skill, particularly the *labor limae,* important for Lattoni. In the last thirteen years of his life, when the rhetoric of civic poetry becomes less pronounced his patriotism acquires undeniable human truth and existential weight. The melding of his love for Italy and Canada constitutes the most evident merit of his writing. To live a dual life in only one existence has been the late but profound discovery of the man and the artist who was Liborio Lattoni. This is the legacy that he has left for future generations: the search to give his life meaning as a father, a believer and a citizen.

It is not an exaggeration to say that from 1915 to 1958 Liborio Lattoni was the most important Italian language writer in Canada. Since the 1930s several Canadian critics, among them W. Kirkconnell who translated into

English selections of his poetry, consider Lattoni "the most outstanding Italian poet in Canada."

Mario Duliani's *La Ville sans femmes*

Mario Duliani was born in Pisino (Istria) in 1885.[9] At the age of seventeen he began writing for the Milan daily *Il Secolo,* which three years later sent him to Paris to manage its Paris bureau. He lived in the French capital until 1936 when, at the urging of the former Canadian ambassador Eugène Berthiaume, he moved to Montreal. For a time he wrote for *La Presse,* while contributing to almost all the French-language publications in the province. His role as a journalist in the *L'Illustration nouvelle,* which later became the daily *Montreal Matin,* was significant in relating for the Italian Canadian public Italy's military campaign in Ethiopia in 1936.[10]

Although he became director of the Italian weekly newspaper *La Verità,* Duliani's true passion was theatre. In 1937 he became the director of the French-language division of the Montreal Repertory Theatre, a professional English-language theatre company founded four years earlier by Martha Allen. According to Quebec actress, the late, Yvette Brind'Amour, the role that Duliani played in the birth of professional French theatre in Canada has been of primary importance.

> In 1936, when he arrived in Montreal, the only professional theatre company in the city was the Montreal Repertory Theatre. He was acquainted with its director, Martha

Allen, and with her support he founded a French "section." Being new to the city, he set out to search for young actors by placing ads in the papers. That is how I got my start at the age of seventeen . . . Duliani had incredible dynamism and enthusiasm! He had such faith in the existence and viability of French Canadian theatre that he succeeded. He gave all the people here confidence. He managed to raise some money and founded a professional theatre company. He was exceedingly charming. He wasn't necessarily physically attractive, but his penetrating gaze revealed much about his intellectual capacity. He was of medium height, with an Italian accent. But he spoke French marvelously. When he arrived in Montreal he was divorced. he lived with the actress Andrée Basillières and, in 1940, before he was arrested, he married Henriette Gaultier, a rather corpulent woman, very distinguished, who left him during his internment.[11]

A brilliant writer, his common, everyday French enjoyed mass appeal.[12] In 1961 at the age of seventy-six, he was the first Italian Canadian to be appointed member of Le Conseil des Arts du Québec — recognition for his rich contribution to the performing arts. Bon vivant, good friend, *à la main,* he had an easy pen and a brilliant mind. Despite his brilliant theatrical career, Duliani is best remembered for his romanticized account as a prisoner of war in the Canadian internment camps of Petawawa and Fredericton during World War II. *La Ville sans femmes* was published in Montreal in 1945, following Duliani's release. (It was subsequently translated into Italian by the author and appeared under the title *La Città senza donne.*) Described by the author as *un documentario romanzato* of his life as a political prisoner, the volume is an account of the daily life of several hundred men of diverse nationalities and of different social classes in the two internment camps the Canadian government had set up in Ontario and New Brunswick. The ethnic diversity of the prisoners is described by Duliani as a tower of babel. In the preface to the book the author writes: "Among the internees that were my companions in the two camps, sixteen nationalities were represented. They were men of every age, from eighteen to seventy-five years. They belonged to every social condition, from the millionaire to the beggar; from every moral level, from the priest to the gangster." *La Ville sans femmes* deserves careful analyses because of the legal, political, existential, and aesthetic tangle of questions it raises.

As a prisoner's journal, *La Ville sans femmes* abounds with *petites histoires* or side stories, often comical in nature, which are the expression of the author's sardonic and affable, but also psychologically sharp temperament. Duliani's objective as a writer was to capture the normality of life with the fewest number of words and the greatest amount of expression. This was the notable feature of the dialogues in his theatre and the collection "Historiettes" in the book *Deux heures de fou rire*. In *La Ville sans femmes* it is the side stories which give vivacity to the text and artistic value to it as literature. They capture succinctly some salient traits of the human soul. Duliani focuses his attention, for example, on the phenomenology of the absence of love among the internees, rather than attempting to delve into the prisoners' souls. Love is presented as a spiritual need, no doubt, but also and more importantly, as linked to "organic laws that will remain for as long as man will live; the pain of love understood in its physical sense, as lust, that will make man moan no matter what his age, and no matter under what conditions he may live."

But although the absence of and need for Woman, as well as the need for love, is crucial to Duliani's book, the central theme of *La Ville sans femmes* is political and deals obviously with the issue of the arrest and internment. The crucial questions; did the arrested Canadian "enemy aliens" of Italian origins truly constitute a threat to Canada's national security? Did they betray Canada? Duliani's answer to these questions is an emphatic no. The internees had committed no reprehensible deeds, nor did they have any intentions of doing so. The physical absence of women acquires a much more profound significance when it is juxtaposed against the internees' loss of freedom, for it becomes the tangible proof of their guilt, of being traitors of their country. The political events cause in them, as Duliani points out, a deep moral disquietude, much more difficult to bear because of the awareness that they are in fact innocent. The internees sole guilt is that of having publicly expressed sympathy with the Mussolini regime prior to the start of the war. At the moment of the declaration of war between Italy and Canada, this sympathy is interpreted at best as suspicious, at worst as leading to treason, sabotage, and terrorism.

Since there has been "guilt," Duliani notes, a price needs to be paid even though the actions of the Italian Canadian internees were not motivated by any deep-felt ideological considerations.

> They are good-natured people, and most of them are of average or less than average refinement. They have been the victims of that need to externalize typical of southern Latins. A parade wearing a black shirt . . . the waving of a flag . . . the giddiness produced by a speech at the end of a banquet . . . the pleasure of seeing one's name printed in a newspaper . . . These are, more or less, all the reproaches that can be made to the internees of the camp.

The Canadian Minister of Justice at that time, Ernest Lapointe, did specify that the civilian internees had been detained, not because they had committed acts of violence but "only because they were viewed as susceptible of committing them." For Duliani, this clarification has a dual function of fundamental importance: it confirms the innocence of the internees, while providing the justification for the federal government's actions as being motivated by national security. It was a matter of principle. Because of the unwritten rules of war, the Italian Canadians became guilty by association, even though they had not committed any crime. There fate was determined by Mussolini's declaration of war on Canada. Duliani repeats often in *La Ville sans femmes* the notion that "if Rome had maintained its neutrality, Italy would have acquired in time an enormous prestige. Italy's international image was subjected to a profound change after only a few months as Germany's ally. Shortly after entering the war, Italy was belittled, humiliated, defeated."

In the chapter "Gli Italiani d'America," which does not appear in the French version of the book, Duliani addresses the international political situation and expresses his own deep anti-Germanic feelings. On June 10, 1940, the day of the declaration of war on France, Great Britain, and Canada, according to Duliani "a crime was committed that must be marked as a black day in the history of humanity." As "a francophile and a humble servant of a Latin ideal," he refused to believe, until the very last moment, "in a war between brothers," that is between France and Italy. The Germans were to Duliani a people that allowed themselves to be perverted by bad philosophers, and tried with Hitler's National Socialism a tragic experiment; as radical and as profound as Luther's Reformation, but based on race instead of religion, though with the same desire for domination. The Germans are "a hardworking people, but they are misguided by the theories of their philosophers and their politicians. A German taken by himself, is a kind and courteous person. But two Germans are already a little Germany and then become unbearable."

The lack of sympathy between Italian and German internees manifests itself in the frequent confrontations between them, even though, in Petawawa and Fredericton, they are internees of two allied countries and are suffering the same unjust fate. Seemingly generated by the living conditions, this animosity is in fact, argues Duliani, motivated by the profound difference of character and conceptualization of life. "Whether it is because of the food or for the discipline, the contrasts are evident. How can I put it? These contrasts between the nationals of the two countries seem to symbolize the great drama of Italy in a war which is taking place across the ocean."

How does Mario Duliani explain his personal condition as a prisoner of war? The arrest of the "enemy aliens" decreed by the federal government is, in his opinion, an abuse of power. But it is a necessary act of control for the welfare of all. In the equation between common good and private justice, Duliani sides with the common good, even though the single citizen will suffer abuse as a result. Duliani compares his period of internment to the time necessary for a customs agent to verify the luggage of a suspect. Once the verification has taken place, if the traveler has nothing to hide, he can go on his way and does not feel animosity towards the officer.

Can one accuse, as has been done, Duliani's line of reasoning as fake patriotism and facile opportunism?[13] With Duliani we are dealing with a complex and multifaceted figure. Historians like Roberto Perin, Luigi Bruti-Liberati, and anti-Fascist journalist Antonino Spada have categorically labeled him a paid informer of OVRA (Opera Vigilanza Repressione Antifascismo), the secret police of the Fascist regime. Their judgment is based on the inclusion of Duliani's name on the list of Fascist secret police operatives published in the supplement of the *Gazzetta Ufficiale* on July 2, 1946.[14]

Although this document is official, it cannot be deemed reliable for at least two reasons. First of all, the files in the Italian archives containing the names of the anti-Fascists and the informers in Canada were compiled in a shoddy manner and contain many lacunae. Often, the inclusion of a name in the list corresponded to the opinion that the consul or the consular clerk had of a person, and to the usefulness or the danger that such a person constituted for the regime. It is undeniable that Mario Duliani, from 1936 to 1940, because of the intellectual preeminence he enjoyed among Italians, did have contacts with consuls like Brigidi or De Simone, and while speaking with them he may have expressed opinions or judgments on anti-Fascists like Spada. But, in so doing, did he really act as a spy, as a paid informer? One must give him the benefit of the doubt, especially if one considers how Duliani earned a living. In the four years before his arrest, Duliani did not need money from the Italian consulate to make ends meet. Until June 1940, the date of his arrest and internment as an enemy alien, Mario Duliani had played a major role in the French-Canadian theatrical scene as well as working as a journalist.[15]

Another reason which challenges the commonly accepted historical opinion is the facility with which a person's name could find itself on the list of OVRA informers, often without the bearer of the name even knowing it. Such was the case, for instance, with Dr. Salvatore Mancuso, one of the leading members of Montreal's Italian community in the 1930s and 1940s. His name was on the official OVRA list, yet he knew nothing of it. More importantly, he never considered himself an informer. Whether or not Duliani was a member of the Fascist secret police remains an open question. What must be underlined, though, is that the official historical record is not very reliable, and therefore one cannot be unequivocal in condemning Duliani.

It appears to me that Duliani's reasoning is the sincere expression of a "new man" who, having gone through a traumatic and painful experience, has acquired an awareness of the intricate rapport that in wartime exists between society and the single citizen. Mario Duliani's forty months of internment were a process of maturation, both human and political. The fruit of his new awareness is to be found in his book *La Ville sans femmes*. Though theatre and journalism remained Duliani's main interest and passion for his entire life, the literary and historical significance of this volume cannot be diminished. It is unquestionably the most passionate account prior to the 1970s on the psyche of Italians in Canada.

Duliani's last years were spent in solitude, in bad health, and destitution. So far no studies exist on Duliani's place and role as a theatre director, and his extensive production as a journalist has never been compiled. When future scholars write the history of Italian Canadian literature, Mario Duliani should occupy a central position as pioneer. He was, with Liborio Lattoni, the most important figure of Italian Montreal's literary reality between the 1930s and 1950s.

When, in 1961, he was appointed by the Quebec government as a member of the Conseil des Arts du Québec, Duliani was truly touched because he saw in this appointment a token of appreciation for a long and distinguished career. Nevertheless, this did not improve his dire economic situation; he died sick, alone, and almost forgotten three years later.

Giose Rimanelli's *Biglietto di terza*

An important contribution to the sparse corpus of Italian Canadian literature prior to the 1970s is the work of Giose Rimanelli. Although recognized primarily as a novelist, Rimanelli has delved into the short story form, verse, travelogues, and autobiographical pieces. His writing is frequently reflective and characterized by a generous measure of symbolism.

One early novel in particular captures our attention for the purposes of the current discussion. *Biglietto di terza* (Third-Class Ticket, 1958) was inspired by Rimanelli's experiences as an immigrant to Canada during the 1950s. It relates in a candid style the tribulations of a cultured Italian man who arrives in Montreal in the 1950s at the height of the immigration boom only to come face to face with unemployment. Finally landing a job as the editor of a weekly Italian-language newspaper, he learns first hand the manner in which the established Italian Canadian elite, the *prominenti,* brazenly exploit the newly arrived immigrants. Disenchanted with his new life and his new home, the character moves from place to place and from one menial job to another; picking tobacco on a farm in Southern Ontario, waiting tables at the Ritz Carlton Hotel.

Coming to terms with the impossibility of finding a place for himself in the new country, the character (and by extension the author) justifies his decision to return to Italy at the end of the novel in the following manner:

> Canada has vast horizons, prairies, forests, and tundra; Canada is the universe; it is the world of tomorrow. I say that all men who have suffered, who have been wronged by society and who have faced the hypocrisy of necessity, should come here to become free. But to remain in this land you would have had to burn the bridges with the past, and over your shoulder in the distant shores you must not hear any voices which call your name. To face the inhuman: this is the only law by which one lives here . . . These are sacrifices which only the hardest of men manage to overcome, those who are in search of hope . . . They do well to love this country; it was very generous with their misery. All the other immigrants do just as well to love it; all the immigrants whom Europe's misfortunes thrust upon these shores. Canada only asked them for their arms. But I am already spiritually too old to remain here. So I must leave.[16]

Rimanelli left Canada bound for Italy shortly after completing his novel in the hope of "avoiding the impenetrable darkness of the Canadian winter." He left the land "where he was not able to live, where he could no longer justify his existence." But, as destiny would have it, Rimanelli's departure from the North American continent was only temporary, as some years later he was to establish himself in Vancouver, and subsequently in Albany, New York. More recently he has lived in Pennsylvania and in Florida.

The collection of short stories *Il tempo nascosto fra le righe* (Time Hidden Between the Lines) which appeared in 1986 is proof that the spiritual void, which Rimanelli alludes to and which he had apprehended as an existential angst in the 1950s, is still very present in his work. This anguish is the expression of his human reality as a deracinated person, and it provides the source of his creative output to which he pegs the mythical return to his land of origin.

Rimanelli's novel *Benedetta in Guysterland* was originally written in English in 1970, but it was not published until 1993. The author has described the work as a *romanzo liquido* — a liquid novel. It is an experimental book with respect to form; a collage and a parody of various levels of language used in North America — from common everyday slang to the language of daily newspapers and magazines, television, books, songs, and the specialistic jargon of the intellectual elite. Acting like the skilled musician that he is, Rimanelli sounds the language out, playing it by ear, holding up to ridicule different aspects of the American way of life, from the ephemeral to the most profound.

Benedetta in Guysterland can be seen as a paradigmatic example of postmodernist writing, both because it is a book assembled from other books and, thus, the cultural product of intersecting cultures, and because the world it describes is always perceived from a distance with a sense of irony. The outcome is a portrait which overturns the American system of values and challenges the social order on which this system is based. In Rimanelli's novel, gangsters are transformed into philosophers who use language cleverly and seditiously, while philosophers, because of their mental congeniality, come to form "families" and behave like bullies or true *mafiosi* in an effort to defend their niche. This very bitter criticism of the American literary and intellectual world does not come as a surprise from the author of *Il mestiere del furbo* (The Cunning Man's Tools, 1959), a caustic panegyric of the obsequious and conformist nature of the Italian intellectual nomenklatura of the 1950s. This is a topic which Rimanelli explored further in 1975 in his novel *Accademia* (1998).

"By incorporating Americans' obsession with the Mafia, sex, and violence, *Benedetta in Guysterland* relates in an unusual linguistic fashion America's rapport with Italy, transforming the stereotypical Italian-American 'mobster-smoothie' into a vital socio-political parody which reveals that, when juxtaposed, sex and violence are clearly each other's complement," writes Pietro Corsi. With this novel, which received the American Book Award for 1994, "Rimanelli has not only gained a place in North American literature, but more importantly he has transcended easy labeling as an Italian, an American, or an Italian American writer to earn a place in the tradition which has created the likes of Kafka, Nabokov, Borges, and Garci Marques."[17]

The intellectual pilgrim that Giose Rimanelli has become, nonetheless, requires roots, not so much physical (for these would be too confining for an explorer and world traveler such as he) but perhaps spiritual ones. He finds the roots he is seeking in his native village of Casacalenda in the Molise region of south-central Italy, as expressed in his memoirs *Molise Molise,* inspired by his trek on motorbike across six thousand kilometers of Italian territory.

According to Rimanelli every voyage is an epic. What matters in the end is not the land upon which one sets foot, but the adversities that must be overcome to get there. This is the reason the character of Ulysses in Dante's *Inferno* believes that "returning does not mean remaining. To embrace and experience the problems of the land, the span of the brief encounter (or re-encounter) means becoming once again a grain of one's land. Roots sprout again, slowly, but deeply; then they shrivel again. Nonetheless, to not be present no longer corresponds to being absent."[18]

The most sophisticated expression of the mythological and epic dimensions that Giose Rimanelli ascribes to his land of origin is to be found in the collection of poems entitled *Moliseide*. The volume contains about one hundred poems written alternately in Italian and in the Molisan dialect with a sprinkling of English, French, Spanish, Albanian, and Ukrainian. The protagonist of these musings is no longer the historical Molisan — the proud and indomitable Samnite sphered/warrior described by the Roman Livy — but the contemporary Molisan, the migran "who comes to understand the world from direct experience and pays dearly for it . . . For the author-traveler epic is a state of mind which juxtaposes real and imagined plains. These ballads and songs are spiritual chapters of an epic-picaresque *Moliseide* of the spirit that the auto-traveler has gathered within the linguistic possibilities of a lyrical/oral narrative, approximating the levels of his human and intellectual experience. To sing about Molise means to speak about ourselves in the most intimate of nuances: as vagabonds and nostalgics, as builders of skyscrapers and temples of learning to thinking labourers of savoir-vivre. If *The Aeneid* sings of glory, then we sing of our everyday passion: of love, pain, anger, conflict, reconciliation, villainy, the distant homeland, dream, desire, ghosts — in order not to create immortal art as Virgil did (almost impossible in today's post-modernist age, as it has ironically been dubbed) — but pop-mush. This, too, can save the memory of one's roots.[19]

The author and the wanderer in Rimanelli sing about love and despair for people and lands which welcome him or about women who love him or who merely smile at him. By singing he comes to know the object about which he sings, and in so doing he reconciles reality and dream.

Pietro Corsi's *La Giobba*

It is easy to see in hindsight that Pietro Corsi's writings belong to the body of Italian Canadian literature as much for their literary value as for their historical relevance as pertains to the question of Italian immigration to Canada during the post-World War II period. Corsi's accounts are significant for at least two reasons. First, they challenge the belief that Canada was a country of unlimited freedoms and opportunities. The country is shown instead as a land where many immigrants had to endure abuses and humiliations. In addition, through his unaffected style, Corsi is the first to identify the spiritual void of "the voiceless people," a theme reclaimed in the 1970s by the new generation of Italian Canadian writers. Rimanelli and Corsi were among the first who tried to relate to and explain the trauma and the difficulties of the immigrant experience in a creative fashion for both an Italian and a Canadian audience.

Before leaving Italy at the end of the 1950s, Corsi had worked as a translator in the film industry in Rome, and as a producer of radio programs in collaboration with Michele Gualdieri. His radio credits include shows such as *Sorella Radio, Orfeo al Juke-Box, Trasmissione domenicale per gli automobilisti,* and the first two editions of *Cantagiro d'Italia.* Corsi settled in Montreal in 1959 where he took the job of editor-in-chief of the Italian-language weekly *Il Cittadino canadese.* His first book *La Giobba* (The Job, 1965, 1982), appeared in installments in the above-mentioned newspaper in the early 1960s. The volume comprises two long stories. The first recounts in a pathetic tone the delusions and humiliations suffered by a poor Italian peasant, Onofrio Annibalini, who is conned by a *padrone* (job agent). He realizes, only too late, that the job he has been promised in Montreal, and for which he paid handsomely, does not exist. The second story, instead, recounts the way power is exercised Mafia-style by a prominent member of the Italian community, who uses any means, however illicit, to get himself elected to Montreal's city council.

In his analysis of *La Giobba,* the American critic Fred L. Gardaphé places the book within the context of the Italian American literary tradition where sociological concerns are highlighted. The economic and political issues raised in the two short stories and their argumentative tone evoke a social situation similar to the one prevailing in the United States in the 1930s, of which the novel *Christ in Concrete* by Pietro Di Donato is a good example. Gardaphé also sees similarities between *La Giobba* and another popular Italian American novel *Wait Until Spring, Bandini* by John Fante. Both works address the issues of the search for employment, survival, and human dignity among Italian immigrants in North America.

But the similarities between Corsi's *La Giobba* and other Italian-American novels end there. Giose Rimanelli is right in pointing out that: "Onofrio Annibalini was born in Italy and emigrated to Canada after World War II. He spoke neither English nor French, only the Molisan dialect. This is in contrast to the characters in Di Donato and Fante, who were born in America before World War II and who behave as Americans, occasionally using Italian phrases and proverbs that their parents taught them."[20]

The deep friendship between Rimanelli and Corsi, as well as their common origin, place Rimanelli in a unique position to interpret the existential and mythological layers of meaning present in Corsi's narrative. Rimanelli writes: "His are works about migration, about the Italian who journeys to distant lands from his ancient native village. Although each of the lands he discovers — Canada, the United States, Mexico — is different in language and culture, all retain the same meaning and wear the same face: darkness at first, light afterwards. They are thus transformed into a mental revolution and become a fairy tale. They act as a bridge, as a sacred bloodline between Europe and America, between humanism and adventure, between meta-science and meditation."[21]

Pietro Corsi's narrative, regardless of whether one labels him Italian, Italian Canadian, Italian American, or even Italian Mexican, is exemplary in its facility to draw from the imagery of a variety of physical and spiritual realities, yet always remaining tied to the memory of his homeland. This is evidenced in Corsi's recent work *Il morbo dell'ozio* (The Sickness of Idleness, 1994), which tells the story, in a style reminiscent of Camus' *The Plague*, of the destruction of a town.

Nowadays, Corsi lives, as he puts it, in pursuit of the sun — in Mexico during the winter, in California during spring and fall, and in Italy, during the summer. His novels include *Ritorno a Palenche* (Return to Palenche, 1985), *Un certo giro di luna* (A Certain Twist of the Moon, 1987), *Lo sposo messicano* (The Mexican Bridegroom, 1989), *Amori tropicali di un naufrago* (The Tropical Romances of a Shipwreck, 1991), and *Il morbo dell'ozio.* His novels, soon to be published, are *L'amapola della Sierra Madre* (The Growing Fields of the Sierra Madre), which is set in Mexico and explores different facets of the cultivation of poppies used to make heroin, and *La matriarca di Fonte del Lupo* (The Matriarch of Fonte Del Lupo) set in the Molise region of Italy.

Tonino Caticchio's *La Scoperta der Canada*

Tonino Caticchio was born in the central south region of Molise, Italy in 1930, but at the age of six was sent off to private school in Rome. There he developed a great love for the eternal city and for everything Roman, which lasted his entire life. In addition to the attachment he felt for his adopted city, Caticchio loved books, popular music, and fine food.

Shortly after arriving in Canada in 1957, he went to work at the Beauchemin bookstore in Montreal. However, writing was his passion, and before long he was writing lyrics to popular songs. He contributed greatly to the success, during the 1960s, of singer Tony Massarelli. For some fifteen years Caticchio played a significant role on the Quebec popular music scene by writing the music and the lyrics in French to over one hundred songs.

Following his success in the pop-music business, Caticchio concentrated his efforts strictly on poetry, using a witty style, ironic twists and simple but colorful language which managed to express life's deeper meanings. His favourite weapon was the sonnet, which he handled with great skill and dexterity. One need only recall the collection entitled *La Scoperta der Canada* (The Discovery of Canada) written in Roman dialect (modeled after *La*

Scoperta de l'America by the late nineteenth-century Italian poet Pascarella). In his collection Caticchio recounts with incisive wit Giovanni Caboto's discovery of Newfoundland in 1497 and Jacques Cartier's arrival in the Indian village of Hochelaga (Montreal) in 1534.

A parody of the *trasteverino* — the typical Roman bully who settles accounts with fist and knife — is the subject of *Rugantino: Storia della maschera romana* (Rugantino: History of a Roman Mask), Caticchio's second volume which appeared in Montreal in the mid 1970s. His third collection is entitled *Storia di Roma ariccontata da mi nonno Pippa* (A History of Rome as Told by My Grandfather Pippa). Here, too, the story is presented from the point of view of simple folk, where a sequence of misunderstandings make for some very hilarious situations. In one sonnet, Grandfather Pippa, who is of Molisan origin, draws a parallel between a historic event and a soccer game. In the same way that during the Italic Wars the Romans suffered a humiliating defeat at the hands of the Samnites, similarly and surprisingly the first-division Roma soccer team is defeated in a come-from-behind win by the amateur-level team from Campobasso.

Caticchio's most significant work is *Ma chi me l'ha fatto fà* (Why Did I Bother) which was published posthumously in Montreal in 1989 thanks to the interest of his close friends. This collection of poems, a testament to the man as a human being and as an artist, can easily be seen as the mature expression of the artist at work. *Ma chi me l'ha fatto fà* contains the most profound expression of his sardonic outlook on human behaviour married to an Epicurean lifestyle. It is Caticchio as a skeptical follower of any ideological diktat, as a loving husband and father, as a complex and tormented human being, and as a skillful poet that emerge from the collection. It should be considered one of the best works by an Italian Canadian poet. Tonino Caticchio died of a heart attack in Montreal in 1985.

Ermanno La Riccia's Short Stories

Among Canadian writers of Italian origin who still use Italian as the language of their literary creation is Ermanno La Riccia. The son of peasants, La Riccia earned a pre-university diploma before immigrating to Canada in the late 1950s where he continued his studies, obtaining a degree in mechanical engineering. Aside from his job as an engineer at Pratt & Whitney, La Riccia has worked as a journalist for Montreal Italian language weeklies such as *Il Corriere italiano* since his arrival in Canada. He has also written for the Italian Catholic monthly *Il Messaggero* published in Padua.

In 1984 La Riccia published with *Il Messaggero* a collection of twenty-three short stories entitled *Terra mia* (Homeground). The underlying themes in the stories can be classified within the ranks of the broad genre of literary realism. More precisely, *Terra mia* can be linked to the *verismo* style of the late nineteenth century, and even more closely to the neorealism of the post World War II period.

There seems to be, purposely or not, a very close similarity between the title story "Terra mia" (the most interesting story in the volume) and "La roba" (Lust For Property), the famous story by Giovanni Verga, the master of *verismo*. La Riccia's stories may seem somewhat anachronistic to contemporary readers for they present an image of a backward, agricultural, poor, working class, still underdeveloped Italy — a country portrayed as a mere source of able bodies to be sent to work overseas.

Throughout the 1960s and 1970s Italy underwent, in the words of Pier Paolo Pasolini, an anthropological revolution. The country gained membership among the world's most industrialized countries, but this also resulted in excessive consumerism and a loss of fundamental spiritual values. Attachment to the Christian heritage is the leitmotif in the collection by La Riccia. It is the Christian virtues of faith, hope, and charity which give the book a solid underlying structure. Equally important in the collection is the recurring theme of the irreconcilable conflict between the desire to return to one's country of origin and the underlying knowledge (more or less accepted) that this has become impossible.

The characters in *Terra mia* are uprooted men and women who live life on a simple track. On one side is day-to-day reality as experienced in the various countries where they have emigrated; on the other is the all-consuming nostalgia for the land and family left behind.

Going back is a constant, indelible wish for them; but going back, they inevitably realize, is impossible. If such a feat is attempted, as in the case of Michelantonio the main character in the story "Terra mia," it does not provide a solution to his existential search. Disillusioned after so many years of living in Canada, but driven by the thought of finding peace of mind by acquiring "that house in the olive grove facing the sea," he must finally come to terms with the fact that only by living with his wife and children born and raised in Canada can he truly be happy. It is neither material things nor his return as a mature adult back to the womb of his native land which can assuage Michelantonio's fears. Once the umbilical cord connecting one to the land of one's birth has been cut, it becomes necessary, in the words of Tennyson's Ulysses, to ". . . become part of all that I have met . . ." In other words the consolation archetype is nothing but the existential component of a person's reality, and reality must be accepted for what it is or what it has become.

Unfortunately, few of the characters in *Terra mia* embody this existential complexity. Their nostalgia is suffocating for both themselves and the reader, their yearning to go back cannot be circumvented. Thus, the immigrant's complex identity, his existential schizophrenia, and his unsolvable problems become too predictable. Equally dissonant is the way in which all the characters resignedly turn to religion as a solution to their problems. Faith, as it is presented, ends up being a practice which does not constitute a plausible solution to the characters' tragic fate.

La Riccia's second volume entitled *Viaggio in paradiso* (A Trip to Paradise), published in 1992 again by *Il Messaggero* in Padua is more of the same, both in form and content. One encounters themes similar to the ones in the first collection with similar strengths and weaknesses.

In many ways Ermanno La Riccia remains a voice in Italian Canadian literature typical of the "older" generation, among whom one finds the likes of Maria Ardizzi, Matilde Torres and Gianni Grohovaz in Toronto; Camillo Carli, Dino Fruchi, Tonino Caticchio and Corrado Mastropasqua in Montreal; and Romano Perticarini in Vancouver — writers whose preferred language of expression is Italian and whose themes attempt to reconcile the paradox of living a dual existence during one lifespan.

The Poets of the *Cenacolo Symposium*

Although not included by Fulvio Caccia in his volume *Sous le signe du phénix (Interviews with the Phoenix,* translated by Daniel Sloate*)* the contribution to the budding Italian Canadian literature by the poets who, at the beginning of the 1970s, came together to form the poets' circle known as the Cenacolo Symposium, cannot be overlooked. The best result of the gatherings is an anthology of poems by Umberto Taccola, Romano Perticarini, Giovanni Di Lullo, and Corrado Mastropasqua. Umberto Taccola was born in Livorno and came to Canada in the early 1950s. He lived in Montreal for over twenty years before moving back to Italy (Isernia), where he still lives. The material and metaphorical humus of his poetry is the preservation and integrity of the peasant world, a reverential attitude towards unspoiled nature, and the redemption of the disenfranchised of the Third World. This theme is manifest in his volume entitled *Una scatola di sole* (A Boxful of Sun) which was published in Montreal in 1978. His second volume, *Una scatola di passi* (A Boxful of Steps), expresses by means of strong imagery (as in the first collection) the beauty of the Italian countryside and its unspoiled lifestyle, as they are discovered on foot almost as a Franciscan pilgrimage.

In his volume entitled *Il fuoco della pira* (The Flame from the Pyre) published in Montreal in 1976, Giovanni Di

Lullo expresses his state of being as a young immigrant, who "with eyes shut tight more clearly beholds heights that angst will never reach." In the act of departing, after yet another homecoming, "everything has been left behind except the memories." Quoting T.S. Eliot, the mature adult Di Lullo writes: "The man who returns will have to meet the boy who left." Even more significant is the dedication to his mother: "Man's sentence lies in the memories — gentleness and humiliation." The gentle recollections of the country left behind and the humiliations endured as a young man uprooted from his land are the opposite poles wherein lies his imagery and from which gush forth the metaphors of Di Lullo's poetry. It is unfortunate that a voice capable of expressing such profound sensitivity has been silent after just one collection.

Corrado Mastropasqua, a medical doctor by profession, still writes poetry. He published with Guernica Editions, in 1988, the volume in Italian entitled *Ibrido* (Hybrid). As the title suggests, it is the hybrid nature of his being that constitutes the main theme of his work. Again, the dual nature of a person's life is at the core of his preoccupations.

Romano Perticarini, originally from Fermo in the central Marches region of Italy, moved to Vancouver, after spending several years in Montreal. In the 1970s, he has published two new bilingual collections: *Quelli della fionda* (The Slingshot Kids) and *Via Diaz*. Many of the poems in these two collections are characterized by the juxtaposition of zestful and joyful childhood memories filtered by the awareness of a mature, anguished adult existence in a foreign country that has with the years become accepted as his new homeland. Perticarini skillfully describes in lyrical terms the beauty and majesty of the Canadian west coast.

The Voiceless People Speak Out

Di Cicco's Roman Candles

The majority of Italians living in Canada in the 1950s could well be described as beasts of burden, pioneers with no cultural memory, people only capable of overcoming the elements and surviving the fierce Canadian winter. Their lot is mere economic survival; their only language is silence. As Robert Kroetsch points out: "We haven't got an identity until somebody tells our story. The fiction makes us real."[22] Since the beginning of the 1970s, the task of Canadian writers of Italian origin has been to render real the existential condition of the Italian Canadians.

These writers began first by portraying and analyzing themselves, their parents, and their background but the focal point of their work inevitably turned to the immigrant experience and evolved to the philosophical contrast between the southern Italian rural heritage and the northern urban Canadian reality.

This *prise de conscience* can be traced probably quite precisely to a group of young Italian Canadian intellectuals, most born in Canada, some arriving at a young age, whose writings started to get attention during the 1970s. Among these are Frank Paci, Dino Minni, Pier

Giorgio Di Cicco, Alexandre Amprimoz, Joseph Pivato, Marco Micone, Antonio D'Alfonso, Fulvio Caccia, Mary di Michele, Antonino Mazza, Mary Melfi, and Caterina Edwards. Although most were born in Italy, all were educated and acculturated in Canada and the United States. It is no wonder, then, that the traumas of physical dislocation and psychic scars are ubiquitous in their work. In Italian, French, or English, the recurring themes for about a decade's worth of writings are exile, dislocation, and the superimposition of a rural reality with all its baggage of memories and images of an urban and industrial North American landscape. There follows nostalgia for the land of origin left behind or often mentioned by parents or grandparents, and the all too unrealistic desire to return there. An equally important theme in many of the writers mentioned (Melfi, di Michele, and Micone in particular, and Paci, D'Alfonso, and Edwards to some extent) is the importance of family ties and the conflictual nature of their still typically patriarchal heritage.

Another fundamental concern expressed throughout Italian Canadian literature is the very complex theme of identity. The so-called split personality, that is, the being suspended between two worlds and two value systems is the common denominator in the anthology of poems in English, *Roman Candles* edited by Pier Giorgio Di Cicco and published in Toronto in 1978. This volume marks a watershed in what is now labeled Italian Canadian writing.

This theme is reprised in another anthology, *Italian-Canadian Voices* edited by Caroline Morgan Di Giovanni published in Toronto in 1984. In many ways it is an appropriate complement to Di Cicco's volume. Morgan Di Giovanni widened the thematic content to include poetry, short stories, and chapters of novels, while arranging the material in chronological order to cover a period of almost forty years. Bilingual collections in Italian and French or unilingual French collections were simultaneously being published in Montreal.

In 1983 the bilingual volume *La poesia italiana nel Quebec/La poésie italienne au Québec,* which included the work of eighteen authors, was edited by the late Tonino Caticchio. The same year also saw the publication of *Quêtes: Textes d'auteurs italo-québécois* edited by Fulvio Caccia and Antonio D'Alfonso. They brought together the work of eighteen new authors writing in French.

It is important to note the important role played by the originally Montreal-based Guernica Editions in the growth of Italian Canadian literature. Nearly all authors of any consequence in Italian Canadian literature have been published or republished in translation by Guernica. Among its most notable publications are: *Sous le signe du phénix: Entretiens avec quinze créateurs italo-québécois* (1985; *Interviews with the Phenix,* 1998), edited by Fulvio Caccia; *Contrasts: Comparative Essays on Italian-Canadian Writing* (1985), edited by Joseph Pivato; *Arrangiarsi: The Italian Immigration Experience in Canada* (1990), edited by Roberto Perin and Franc Sturino; and the proceedings of the first convention on Italian Canadian literature held in Vancouver in the fall of 1986 published under the title *Writers in Transition,* edited by Dino Minni and Anna Foschi Ciampolini. Many more titles have been added in the course of the last decade by critics such as Francesco Loriggio, Joseph Pivato, and others.[23]

Fulvio Caccia's *Sous le signe du phénix (Interviews with the Phoenix)* received much critical acclaim. Instead of being the subject of discussion as is often the case, the fifteen authors interviewed in book talk about themselves and their role in Quebec society. They deal with the concept of *culture de convergence,* criticizing the traditional ethnocentric vision of the francophone intelligentsia. They challenge the nationalist Quebecois understanding of a homogeneous Quebecois society which had characterized French-language literature during the Quiet Revolution (1959-1980), as expressed in the writings of the likes of Hubert Aquin, Michèle Lalonde, Gaston Miron, Paul Chamberland, and others. The artists of Italian origin criticize Quebec nationalism as the sole inspiration for artistic creation as abetted by the Parti Québécois when it came to power in 1976. After the defeat of the Parti Québécois in the 1980 referendum on sovereignty-association, the then prevalent restrictive conception of nationalism was shelved and an urgent need arose to see in minority groups and in ethnic difference not a threat but an enrichment to the Quebec and French-Canadian identity. This notion held sway for nearly a decade until a new wave of nationalist fervor manifested itself (which still persists), due to the failed ratification of the constitutional amendments known as the Meech Lake Accord in 1990, the referendum on the Charlottetown Accord in 1992. This culminated in yet another referendum on independence, or to use Jacques Parizeau's phrasing "souveraineté/partenariat" in 1995.[24]

Fulvio Caccia's volume is still significant for it placed itself at the center of the cultural debate on the redefinition of Quebecois identity and on the role that the Italian community (the largest of the minority groups) could have or should have played in the entire process. This is still, by the way, an open question.

Equally significant from an academic perspective was the volume *Contrasts*. In the essay entitled "Ethnic Writing and Comparative Canadian Literature" Joseph Pivato calls for a pluralistic perspective in establishing the parameters of criticism in Canadian literature.[25]

With "Discoverism and Italian-Canadian Historiography" which appeared in *Writers in Transition* I first challenged the notion of "the two founding people" by which the official English and French language historiographies claimed and continue to claim special collective rights based on a person's ethnic origins.

In these writings the logical conclusion is that the anglophone/francophone dichotomy which purports to seek unifying themes either from a federalist or separatist perspective be dismantled. In other words, in terms of history, identity, thematics, mythopoetry, and even geography need to be reconsidered because the result of the English-French vision — be it from a federalist or separatist point of view — grants "the two founding peoples" an indisputable officialdom (and in the case of Quebec) exclusivity with respect to other ethnic groups. The label ethnic writers or users of "non-official" languages translates itself into a policy of exclusion or marginalization, or if a more benign attitude is followed, into an attempt to assimilate them into "official mainstream" Canadian literature which is not interested in "ethnic" issues. In a country of immigrants like Canada, who besides the Native North Americans is not an ethnic?[26]

To try to address the very complicated issues surrounding First Nations, founding peoples, and the multicultural mosaic all at once is a daunting task which goes beyond the scope of this book. However, it cannot be denied that "minority" writers of Italian origin are making a significant contribution to the debate *in fieri* on Canadian identity. Furthermore, since they write in English and French, while still maintaining Italian as the common language or culture, Italian Canadian writers have become the link between the "two solitudes." In the world of Canadian literature and historiography, still characterized by the absence of dialogue between the two official charter groups, this new role constitutes a significant achievement, for no other component of the Canadian population can claim it.

Antonio D'Alfonso
and Guernica Editions

In retrospect, Antonio D'Alfonso can be described as a seminal figure in the birth and dissemination of Italian Canadian literature. Born in 1953 of Italian parents in Montreal where French is the predominant language, D'Alfonso was educated in English from grade school to university. He is the product of an urban, multi-lingual, multi-ethnic reality — the mirror of what contemporary Canada has become. In 1979 D'Alfonso founded Guernica Editions whose primary objectives have been to publish young Canadian writers of Italian origin (in both French and English), to translate well-known Quebecois writers, novelists, and poets into English, and to present *Italianità* as a continental concept which includes Quebecois, Canadian, and American authors. Guernica has also translated German writers of Italian origin, as well as Italian writers into English, to show that minority writing or writing *per se* is an individual and international phenomenon and an inevitable dimension of contemporary literature.

Since its move to Toronto in the early 1990s, Guernica Editions has enriched the concept of "ethnic writing" by providing the critical apparatus which mainstream criticism has neglected. Transcending national boundaries, Guernica Editions is unique; it sees in diversity not a concept to fear but a basic tenet of a postmodern artistic sensitivity.

Though primarily known for his role as a publisher, Antonio D'Alfonso is also an established and prolific author. He began by writing poetry but has turned his attention to novels as well as criticisms in English, French, and Italian. Though his primary language as editor and publisher is English, he has written extensively in French. The multi-faceted nature of D'Alfonso existence, however, does not exclude anguish and a continuous process of search and self-redefinition. On the contrary, it is one of the constituents of his reality, both as an individual and as a writer. His poem entitled "Babel" best exemplifies this linguistic and existential schizophrenia:

> Nativo di Montréal
> élevé comme Québécois
> forced to learn the tongue of power
> vivì en México como alternativa
> figlio del sole e della campagna
> par les franc parleurs aimé
> finding thousands like me suffering
> me casé y divorcié en tierra fria
> nipote di Guglionesi
> parlant politique malgré moi
> *steeled in the school of Old Aquinas*
> queriendo luchar con mis amigos latinos
> Dio where shall I be demain
> (trop vif) qué puedo saber yo
> spero che la terra be mine.[27]

D'Alfonso's existential reality is rich in contradictions; he was an English-language poet (until the mid-1980s) with a Latin sensitivity, surrounded by a French-speaking majority which is itself a minority in an English-speaking country and continent. In such an environment — a Montreal saturated with influences of diverse linguistic realities — D'Alfonso's creativity has thrived in his attempts to overcome the contradictions that surrounded him, something which was and still is not easy to do, be it Montreal or Toronto. Consequently, he has attempted to find a theoretical justification in what he defines as the "triangulation of cultures," among Italian, French, and English.

Such a synthesis is possible for D'Alfonso only if one is able to become essential. Thus, he harks back to a classical view of life where nature and culture become amalgamated, instead of being mutually exclusive. He has always tried to weld his Italian sensitivity of which the migration process is a major component with an environment where French is the language of the abstract and English is the language of the concrete. The joining of different cultural heritages and realities are high on the list of priorities for D'Alfonso the editor, as well as for D'Alfonso the poet, as his most recent works demonstrate. He has translated into French a collection of poems entitled *The Other Shore* (1986) which appeared under the title *L'Autre Rivage* (1987). His novel *Avril ou L'anti-passion* (1990) which originally appeared in French was published in English as *Fabrizio's Passion* (1995). For D'Alfonso writing can be arduous work; being accountable to three cultures is no easy task. In his poetry and fiction he highlights his state as a deracinated person in the constant and vain search of belonging.

In *La Chanson du Shaman à Sedna* (1973), his first collection of poems, which he chose to write in French, the principal theme being explored is rebellion against paternal authority. The story of Sedna, an Inuit girl pursued by her father, acts as a metaphor throughout. To avoid coming to an awful end, Sedna finds refuge at the bottom of the ocean and becomes queen of her people. The shaman is the only being capable of linking earth and sea. For D'Alfonso the shaman is also the symbolic capacity of the poet who by means of words binds the father and the mother figures, and thus overcomes abuse. Poetry, thus, becomes a liberating force, a synthesis between the male and female in nature and in human nature — a more gentle synthesis of what it means to be fully human.

In D'Alfonso's second volume, *Queror* (1979), the break with the father figure continues, but it is the anguish of a lonely man who can find a reason for living only in physical relations which comes through. Passion, sensuality, sex, and the strange sounding structure of sentences characterize the work, which by means of the intermingling of different languages, shatters the syntactic frigidity of much English Canadian poetic output.

Black Tongue (1983) pushes the search for Latin roots even further, both from a thematic as well as a formal point of view. Just like the *foco d'amore* constitutes for Dante the guiding principle through life and through the after life, similarly in D'Alfonso it is love and passion which allow him, however reluctantly, to retrace the path of the immigrant and rediscover the pain of breaking up with his language and country of origin. As the son of immigrants he has a " . . . black tongue, desert of broken bones, tarnished . . .;" and it is with this hybrid tongue that, disheartened, he must reinvent the art of love and being. "To emigrate is possessing the soul of sadness, is to smother the power of the heart." It is through the remembrance of a country lost that D'Alfonso the poet expresses his desire to repossess, to behold a land to love.

This desperate attempt to repossess the motherland is the underlying theme of his volumes entitled *The Other Shore* (1986) and *L'Autre Rivage* (1987). *Italiam non sponte sequor,* he writes, quoting Virgil. The effort centers around an attempt, however desperate, inevitably fragmented and inconclusive, to find in Italian women an emotional pillar capable of consoling the loner, the spiritual vagabond, the eternal pilgrim. The poet's return to his roots seems to restore, temporarily at least, some balance and some much-longed-for peace of mind. In the poem "Italia mea, amore," a cathartic rediscovery of Italy occurs. The young man, who had been "insured . . . reassured . . . fucked" (" . . . enjôlé . . . cajolé . . . enculé . . ."), who had lost his mother tongue and history" and who heard his country of origin referred to as "a whore, / a crook, a drunkard, an addict, / a hypocrite, a terrorist, a religious fanatic," finally has the courage to treat others the way they have been treating him. Only then, after "just one look, one kiss, / one caress, one night beside you, " does he rediscover himself and understand who he really is. Only then does he dare to declare, "Now if they ask me my name, / I take the ink from your earth / and beside Antonio D'Alfonso / I sign *Amore.*" This attainment of inner peace becomes complete, even if only momentarily, in Guglionesi, the small town of his parents and ancestors:

> Je me sens vraiment Italien ici. Mais j'en rougis. On m'a obligé à avoir honte. Au Québec, au Canada on n'a pas le droit d'être ce que l'on est. Je dois m'habituer à être ce que je suis, malgré les critiques qu'on fait à mon égard. [I feel truly Italian here. Yet I feel ashamed. I was made to feel shame for being an Italian. In Quebec, in Canada, we are not allowed to be what we truly are. I must learn to be what I am, despite the criticism.]

For D'Alfonso the rediscovery of one's inner self is directly linked to the rediscovery of one's mother tongue.

> When I write I translate . . . I write with the memory of one language in mind and express this memory in another language. It is the marriage of memories. I cannot write disregarding the Italian words I use to describe to myself the dazzling panoramas of man's command of nature seen from the heights of Guglionesi.[28]

Despite the rediscovery of his existential roots — roots which he carries inside himself indelibly like the colour of his skin, D'Alfonso remains a nomad whose only homeland ends up being his mother tongue, a bastardized mother tongue, but which he nonetheless imparted to his daughter. Once he has left the country of his ancestors, the dilemma of identity resurfaces; and the poet, like a chameleon that changes the colour of his skin, must learn to assume different roles.

> I dress myself up whenever I go out: I use the accepted lingo: I am an Italian Quebecois; I am an Italian Canadian; I am an intellectual; I am nothing at all . . . I carry in me two countries, two Imaginaries. I have no desire to be singular nor plural, no desire to be intercultural nor transcultural. I am dual. 1. Quebecois, with all its connotations; 2. Italian, with all its connotations. I am happy with my imperfect truths and contradictions.

Herein lies the reason D'Alfonso is never at home anywhere: "I am an eternal pilgrim who will never say: *Me voici restitué à ma rive natale.*"

Fulvio Caccia's *Aknos*

Fulvio Caccia was born in Florence in 1952 and emigrated to Montreal with his family in 1959. Contrary to the trend typical of Italian Montrealers, he attended French-language school. His interest in literature manifested itself at a young age. In the 1960s, as a teenager, Caccia read Quebecois poets like Lapointe, Ouellette, Miron and Brault, the major exponents of what can defined as "la réappropriation du territoire" — the cultural component of the wider social and political phenomenon commonly referred to as the Quiet Revolution. Caccia never obtained a university degree; to a large extent he can viewed as a self-taught intellectual. In his twenties he began writing for a number of cultural and literary magazines, among them *Moebius,* and, in 1982, together with Bruno Ramirez, Antonio D'Alfonso, and Lamberto Tassinari founded the transcultural magazine *Vice Versa* which he directed for a while. In 1983 he published his first collection of poems, *Irpinia,* in French. In 1984 he assembled, with Antonio D'Alfonso, the anthology *Quêtes: Textes d'auteurs italo-québécois.* In 1985 he published *Sous le signe du phénix: Entretiens avec quinze créateurs italo-québécois (Interviews with the Phoenix)* and a second collection of poetry, *Scirocco.* In 1989, after living in Montreal for thirty years, he moved to Paris, where he still resides. He teaches Quebecois literature at Université de Nanterre and intercultural relations between francophonie and anglophonie at Université de Paris XII (Villetaneuse). In addition to being a writer and professor, Fulvio Caccia continues to work as a journalist. While residing in Montreal, he was a contributor to *La Presse* and wrote a weekly column two years running for *Le Devoir*. In France he writes for several dailies and magazines, namely *Le Monde diplomatique, L'Évènement du jeudi, Libération* and *Globe-Hebdo*.

In 1994 Caccia published the collection of poems *Aknos* for which he received the Governor-General's Award. The same year he also published in Montreal the collection of short stories *Golden Eighties* and edited with Bernard Hreglich the anthology *Panorama de la poésie contemporaine françaises*. He edited a second anthology of poetry *Atlantis: Poètes du Québec et d'Irlande*. His essay *Cybersexe: Les connection dangereuses* appeared in Montreal and Paris in 1995 followed by another essay entitled *La République Métis*.

A man of varied interests and opinions not to mention a prolific writer, Caccia deserves more than what can be reported in a single chapter. But space being limited, I have chosen to focus attention here only on Caccia the poet. It is through his poetry, I believe, that the multi-faceted Caccia is best observed. Caccia makes this abundantly clear in his volume *Aknos,* for not only is this work the reflection of the mature artist, it is also evidence of the increasingly high quality attained by artists of Italian Canadian origin, whether they are writing in English or French.

Though published in 1994, *Aknos* is the product of the previous fifteen years of writing. The volume contains four collections: two (*Irpinia* and *Scirocco*) as well as part of the third (*Annapurna*) were published previously. The new addition to the work is the collection entitled *Aknos,* which also serves as the book's title. In the Postface Fulvio Caccia traces chronologically and thematically his career as a poet. Through the word "Irpinia," Caccia addresses the immigrant condition and its transformation. This title stands for both a region in southern Italy where massive emigration occurred and the boat by means of which this transhumance took place. As such, the themes of territory and its loss coincide with the themes relevant in Quebec poetry in the late 1950s and 1960s, a period during which Quebec itself was in the process of renaming itself. The struggle to defeat the alienation felt by Quebecois poets like Miron was also felt by Caccia because immigration is a form of otherness. But it is an otherness aware of its own becoming, and this makes it different from the otherness of the colonized mind which discover itself as being colonized before it can be transformed into an affirmation, into a positive concept. By switching the theme from country to woman to love, Caccia becomes the image in the mirror that expresses the shattering of identity which frightens many Quebecois writers. The result of Caccia's quest is this: "The result is a journey whose two poles are nostalgia for the country left behind, and torment at the hands of the beloved, with the myth of Lilith as the symbol."[29] Irpinia, the point of departure, is in southern Italy, Naples to be more precise. It is symbolized as "an extravagant old woman from Africa, whose memory is scented with iodine." The point of arrival is Canada, specifically Montreal, where "the secret is shattered on the roads of salt / dazzled by the clarity of the myth." Once the physical journey is over, what remains to be fulfilled is the "persistent dream" nourished by "future fervour."

With *Irpinia,* writes Robert Giroux, "from the beginning of the journey, a wealth of personal imagery is created and an entire rhetoric unfurls around three major themes, or rather three quests: first, the quest for identity which is very important in Caccia's work ('Their accent is veined with foreign inflections'); second, the quest for language of expression ('Mixed-blood North great magnetic force / seducer of languages / you sow the seeds of myth,' and 'tomorrow your tongue will storm the dunes'); and third, but not less important and constantly resurfacing, the quest for love ('I look for your shadow your eyes your pouting lips in the scratched window of winter')."[30]

Land, sea, silence, dreams, alienation, and the continuous search for the myth of America constitute the range and mark the territories and the itineraries. *Irpinia* can be seen as "the crucible in which Caccia's later work ferments and grows."[31]

In the second collection, *Scirocco,* Fulvio Caccia takes his experience of existential transhumance a step further by expressing the conflictual nature of the relationship (love and hate) he has with his native culture. Italy becomes the synonym of the omnipresent mother of Origin, a continuously gushing spring. The central theme of *Scirocco* is the metaphorical return to the country where the hot wind of the desert blows. By so doing, Caccia hopes to symbolically erase the oppressive remembrance of his departure, which explains the title of the first section "Le Voyage blanc." The poet does not return in physical terms, but writes the obituary on his past. The death and expulsion from the author's memory of the desire for the Other is the cathartic objective of the collection so that the author can finally detach himself from the oppressive love by and for the Other. But the Other does not let go so easily; hence, we find in *Scirocco* a series of claims and counter claims, of resistances and deviations. The poet's desire to erase his memories of the ancient Mother (Italy) becomes a duel, and at the same time constitutes the thread for his journey toward liberation. The quest for memory and the search for love also characterize "L'anti-voyage," the second part of *Scirocco*. The price Caccia has to pay for ridding himself of the memory of his original Italian past is the discovery of solitude and sorrow. He discovers the vertiginous void: silence.

In his dialectical approach to the feeling of love Fulvio Caccia tries to unite two contemporary poetical traditions: the Quebecoise and the Italian. The first is evident when he describes Montreal reality and when he alludes the difficult relationship with language. The second is manifest in the imagery and the onomatopoeic power of words such as in the works of poets like Ungaretti, Montale, Saba, Pavese. For instance, many images in *Scirocco* are reminiscent of the dry and barren landscapes so prevalent in Montale's *Ossi di seppia*. By combining these two poetical traditions Caccia is able to reconcile his two *imaginaires,* thus, finding an existential equilibrium, and at the same time establishing a link with the best exponents of contemporary poetry. In *Annapurna* the dilemma of choosing the right words to elevate them to the level of legend and myth is Caccia's primary concern. To transfer one culture into another, to become truly transcultural, becomes a daunting task. Caccia uses French to express an Italian *imaginaire* and to emulate the great models that he absorbs so as to fully rediscover the physical presence that the return journey implies. How can a poet writing in French simplify a language like Italian where assonance and rhyme abound? Caccia says:

> I enjoyed working in a language where the alexandrine's echo is faint but real. I hesitated between using it in a traditional fashion or pushing it to its limits and beyond. I tempered my enthusiasm by imposing on the poems in this collection . . . a certain modern stylistic leanness. I opted for the demands of economy, the desert in its spiritualized form, rather than giving in to facility and fashion. The sirocco, like the ironic tone of *Annapurna,* is the end of the formal itinerary through Italy and the violence of everday living. Amorous adventure then, but a quest for language as well. Words that always vanish just when we attempt to grasp them. Because this poetic language can only come from the *broken ressemblance* with our mother tongue.[32]

In the fourth section of the volume *Aknos,* Fulvio Caccia arrives at a synthesis. The recurring themes in *Irpinia, Scirocco,* and *Annapurna* find their final expression in the images of the delta and the metaphor of dream. In *Aknos* the poet expresses an *imaginaire* where everything comes together in physical, existential and metaphorical terms. Although Caccia mentions the Bible — particularly the Song of Songs and Ecclesiastics — as a source of his inspiration, it is almost impossible, for example, when reading "Poème de la patience," not to be reminded of the poetry of Saint John Perse, namely *Exil* and especially *Anabase*.

Aknos is the story of a physical and spiritual adventure divided into three sections. The adventure begins at five in the afternoon, the moment when day is waning and the night is waxing, where the cycles of night and day intermingle. *Aknos* begins "delta-time, plateau-time from which the poet's words ascend, seeking a singularity of expression between the intimacy of a poetic journal and the lyricism typically associated with love poetry."[33] The delta is a territory swept by wind and waves where deserted flora barely survive. It is there that suddenly a man appears, Aknos. From the margins he wants to form objects in the labyrinth of the delta, while it is being invaded by night and silence. The delta is also a mythic extension of the continent "a stormy labyrinth inhabited by all kinds of erotico-religious fantasies." Aknos wants to abandon the shifting earth to embrace the soul of the delta, and as he walks through it his voice mixes with murmurs. They are the voices of idols buried in the sand, the forced exile of peoples like the ones evoked in the Bible, those searching for the promised land. The crossing of the delta acquires a meaning through the presence of the marshes, the deserted center of the labyrinth. Caught in a blinding maelstrom, Aknos dreams of resurfacing, of regaining speech. But inevitably he goes around in circles and looks for another path to emerge from the marshes so he can once again feel the earth's resistance and rejoin the sleeping girl, the source of his mounting desire. Finally, having enjoyed the fever of dreams, having experienced the joy of sexuality with the woman of the dunes, he is capable of interpreting the dreams and of going back to the continent and to firm footing to live more concretely. For Aknos, epic character and expression of both stoic despair and feverish love, the journey is finally over. But, for Caccia the man, the peace found through words is momentary; his existential odyssey continues.

C. Dino Minni's *Other Selves*

The notion of split identity, so ubiquitous in D'Alfonso's *The Other Shore,* is also the underlying theme in the collection of short stories *Other Selves* by C. Dino Minni. Born in Bagnoli del Trigno in the province of Isernia in 1942, Costantino Dino Minni was raised in Vancouver where his parents immigrated when he was still a young boy. *Other Selves* (1986) consists of seven short stories all of which have first and second generation Italian Canadians as main characters. What they all share is an indelible sense of exclusion, of non-belonging. In the story entitled "Roots" Berto Donati returns to his home town of Villa with his wife in search of the ghost of his childhood self in the hope that by doing so he may appease his existential anguish. But he quickly realizes that the "voyage home" does not give him that spiritual serenity which he longs for. He feels like a tourist and inevitably acts like one — so much so that at the end, as he sips one last glass of wine, he exclaims, "Quite good, but it isn't me!" A similar situation occurs in "El Dorado." During the economic crisis of the 1930s Rocco Sebastiano who had emigrated from Italy becomes Rocky Sebastian in order to improve his chances of finding work. He now lives in an old folks home. He urges his grandson Seb to take a trip back to the old country in order to trace the family tree. It is when young Sebastian visits the old bell factory where his grandfather used to work that he finally understands why his grandfather, though often speaking lovingly of the town, had never wanted to go back.

In "Details from the Canadian Mosaic," Mario, a young immigrant, experiences the alienation typical of those who are marginalized and who must work hard to be accepted in a new environment. He finally succeeds and the acculturation occurs when he becomes a very good baseball pitcher. But the price he must pay is the very transformation of his identity; his name is changed from Mario to Mike. To fit in, he is Mario at home and Mike in the street.

The identity crisis does not just afflict the young. Even the elderly, like Margherita — the archetypal immigrant woman from a peasant background — suffer, though, silently because they feel excluded and misunderstood. Margherita's stoic heroism, exacerbated by her paralyzing accident which left her mute, is not understood nor appreciated by her two well-integrated, English-speaking daughters. Ironically, it is through their dialogues that the reader comes to know and eventually admire Margherita. Although she remained very traditional in her value system, she had shown great courage and steadfastness when she became a young widow. She was determined to work hard, so she could raise and keep her family together. Her younger daughter's criticism rings hollow, especially when the sister points out their mother's resolve and courage. But the generational conflict goes deeper than the typical misunderstanding between parents and children. It is two world views that clash

Ancient Memories, Modern Identities   117

and cannot be reconciled: one from a peasant background and the other from a modern urban reality.

Even when identity is not a constant preoccupation (as it is for the character of Berto Donati who does not know if he is Italian or Canadian and therefore remains on the sidelines of both cultures), the characters in these "ethnic" stories have different emotional reference points as a result of their background. What is it that causes them to be marginalized? It is memory, according to Minni.[34] The writers, men and women, who have a recent history of immigration such as the Italian Canadians, must inescapably come to terms with the issue of self-identity and belonging. This explains why in Minni's stories (as in those of so many others in poems, novels, memoirs, or essays) the "voyage home" to try and recover a part of the self is a constant motif. A return to one's own roots, however, is never easy and does not resolve the ambivalence and the sense of duality which the writers feel. Their life will be dangling between both worlds until death.

Since present-day Canada is inhabited by people the majority of whom have come from other countries, the immigrant experience is according to Minni the common denominator or the glue which keeps the mosaic together: "We are all immigrants within our own country," proclaims Minni.[35]

Yet to be determined is the place that the "ethnic writer" can and must occupy in a multi-ethnic society, in the "cultural mosaic," as present-day Canada is being redefined. If an author such as Minni were to delve into his own ethnic background and culture of origin, to which culture would he belong? Is he Italian or Canadian? Another problem with ethnic labeling is this: Can an "ethnic" writer perceive the life experience of other groups only from the outside looking in? Will he be necessarily superficial or stereotypical in his understanding of otherness? Can or must an ethnic writer belong to the mainstream, to the dominant and official culture in order to count? Minni's answer to these questions is that "in a society that resembles a mosaic we are all ethnics with respect to our neighbors."[36] He concludes by saying that, in the short story genre, the presence of the outsider is a constant whether the author's name is Margaret Atwood, Anne Hébert, or Dino Minni. This particular position, standing outside looking in and seeing reality from a different angle, is present not just in Canadian short stories, but has been a characteristic also in the French *conte,* the Italian *racconto,* the German *novelle,* and the Latin American *cuento.* Minni is convinced that in analyzing their ethnic roots, writers of various origins are contributing to the creation of a new Canadian identity. Renouncing, as they are, a narrow definition of nationalism, these writers are allowing regional cultures to assert themselves, to develop, and to ascend to the level of world literature and therefore to universal themes.

"The process," Minni writes, "makes us more ethnic and at the same time more Canadian. The immigrant perspective found in Italian Canadian stories and other 'ethnic' stories has made us aware of our literary ties with the rest of the world and has, paradoxically, focused attention on the true nature of our own culture."[37] The label "ethnic writer" is not, Minni states, a reductive definition, but simply a sociological category which is useful as a critical tool. It ought not to imply a value judgment. C. Dino Minni is undeniably a Canadian writer. He was raised and educated in Vancouver and worked for over a decade as literary critic for *The Vancouver Sun*. He also edited a collection of short stories by new writers, among them Nino Ricci, entitled *Ricordi* which appeared in 1988. He was also one of the driving forces behind the first national convention on Italian Canadian literature held in Vancouver in September of 1986. He was co-editor (with Anna Foschi Ciampolini) of the proceedings of the conference, later published under the title *Writers in Transition* (1991). C. Dino Minni died in Vancouver at the age of forty-eight.

Marco Micone's Trilogia

Marco Micone is another Italian Canadian, or Italo-Quebecois writer as he prefers to define himself, convinced of the necessity to discuss topics related to the immigrant experience so as to bring about the renewal and enrichment of French-Canadian — or rather — Quebec literature. Born in Montelongo, Italy in 1945, Micone has been living in the heart of Montreal's ethnic neighbourhoods since 1958. He completed his studies at McGill with a thesis on the noted Quebecois playwright Marcel Dubé and has been teaching at Vanier College, an English-language institution where the majority of students is neither of English nor French origin — in other words, most are "ethnics." Remarried to a French-speaking Quebecoise and father of two boys, Micone gained the spotlight at the beginning of the 1970s for his political activism in left-wing causes within the Italian community and also for his support of the Parti Quebecois policies, in particular, the implementation of Bill 101, the French-language charter. Fundamental to Micone's frame of mind is the historical and sociological concept of *culture immigrée* which rests on three supporting planks: life as experienced by immigrants in their country of origin; the emigration-immigration experience, with the deracination, psychological insecurity, and social exploitation which result; the future of society (specifically Quebec) with all the difficulties inherent in integrating immigrants who have been left on the margins of society so far.[38]

Indelibly struck by the trauma of immigration, on one hand Micone's objective has been to break the wall of silence maintained by the Italian community's elite whose interest it is to keep the community stifled, inward-looking, and attached to obsolete folklore; on the other, to shout at francophone Quebeckers about the problems experienced by Italian immigrants (and in general by all other immigrants) and the real causes behind their emigration.

The burden of the marginalization of the entire community, which is carried by "the young people of the second generation, relegated to monoethnic English-language schools in a society where the vast majority is French-speaking," has incited Micone to write for the theatre. Micone's dominant trait as a playwright is an unabashed form of sociological pedagogy which often descends into preachiness. This is evident in the trilogy on immigration which he wrote in the course of the 1980s: *Gens du Silence* (*Voiceless People,* 1982), *Addolorata* (1984), and *Déjà l'agonie* (*Beyond the Ruins,* 1986). This tendency was underlined by English and Italian language media, whereas the French-language public and critics received the trilogy well and have made Micone the best known author of Italian origin in Quebec.

With his plays, Micone tried to give vent to the voiceless people, those whom Giovanni Verga called *i vinti* (the vanquished), the peasant masses in Italy oppressed through time who went on to constitute the proletariat in the cities of North America. The Italian pioneers who Giose Rimanelli described in *Biglietto di terza* as having no conscience and no cultural memory — who only expressed themselves through their silence — are the protagonists of Micone's theatre. Micone wants to serve a didactic purpose for the urban villagers whose only ambition seems to be to stave off atavistic hunger and to assimilate a consumerist and petit-bourgeois system of values imposed upon them by unscrupulous notables.

In the artistic philosophy of the Miconian universe one finds a will and a heritage that is both enlightened and palingenetic. Generosity, sincere love, and respect for the dignity of the illiterate masses permanently excluded from the bourgeois heritage of traditional Italian culture are the elements which spur him to give a voice to *les gens du silence* (the voiceless people). The humus or direct link between Italian culture and Micone's art is the neorealistic aesthetic and above all its ideological presuppositions and historical corollaries: anti-Fascism; the *nazionale-popolare* matrix inspired by the Marxist thinker Antonio Gramsci. The themes Micone delves into are the neglect of the peasant world ravaged by emigration and the guilt he assigns to the Italian political class, in particular the postwar Christian Democrats. It is no accident that Micone teaches the history of immigration and knows the *questione meridionale* (the southern Italian question) very well.

It is rather easy to discern in Marco Micone's theatre echoes of the social and political realism found in Bertolt Brecht or in Dario Fo (the contemporary Italian Marxist playwright who won the Nobel Prize in 1998). It is important to keep this in mind because in both *Gens du silence* and *Addolorata* the dramatic technique adopted by the author tends to mimetically reproduce on the stage the daily life of the Italian Canadian, but with a grotesque sneer when it comes to their behaviour, and with a high degree of exaggeration when their consumerist and patriarchal value system is portrayed.

This brings to mind, for instance, the dominating and psychologically brutal relationship that Gino maintains with Addolorata. Equally significant is the naiveté and alienation displayed by Addolorata, who deludes herself into believing she can overcome her problems and make it socially as a woman by learning to speak, however approximately, four languages.

The characteristic element of Micone's theatre, apparent in his first two plays, is a clear, sometimes tedious, desire to teach by way of his very considerable mimetic capability in psychological as well as linguistic terms. His characters are made to use *joual* (colloquial Quebec French), English, and Italian expressions, often swear words. The merit of Micone's art, however, lies in the author's ability to put on the stage the ephemeral and fatuous nature of the values being pursued; the age old oppression of woman doubly alienated (for she is both an immigrant and woman), and the insoluble drama of existence in constant struggle between the Italian peasant heritage and the urban North American reality where human beings exist as proletarians to be exploited.

What happens when the theatre of everyday life and social criticism aspires to become an art form where remembrance and metaphor become the dominant trait, as is the case with Micone's third play *Déjà l'agonie (Beyond the Ruins)*? The result is a plunge into worn out metaphors and lack of verisimilitude: serious flaws for a theatre which has its raison-d'être in realism.

Beyond the Ruins contains two plot lines; the first, set in Quebec, describes the reasons there is no understanding between Luigi and his wife Danielle and between the son and his parents. (This is the more convincing of the two plots.) The other plot line is set in Montelongo, where grandfather, father, and son meet and assess the course of their lives only to discover the emptiness of their existence. This part of the play is rather weak. Recycled metaphors which lack semantic freshness abound and are often nothing more than bookish reminiscences taken from veristic and neorealistic novels and short stories. In *Beyond the Ruins* the historical analysis from a Gramscian perspective is discordant when juxtaposed to the fatalism of the metaphorical vocabulary being used by the characters. In conclusion, Micone is very persuasive when he writes theatre which is more or less a form of sociological dialogue, but demonstrates the limitations of his inspiration when he aspires to write plays where remembrance and metaphors should enliven and enrich the plot line.

Towards the end of the 1980s, after the fall of the Berlin wall and the subsequent crisis of the Marxist ideology, Micone's discourse softened. Nevertheless, this did not bring about a decrease in the number of his public appearances on social and political issues, namely those concerning the secession of the province of Quebec from the rest of Canada. The failure of the Meech Lake and Charlottetown constitutional propositions, in 1990 and 1992 respectively, gave momentum to the French-speaking secessionist forces in Quebec. Micone agrees with them, believing that Quebec's distinctive culture cannot thrive and its economic imperatives are unattainable within Canada, and are even incompatible with those of the rest of the country. For him Quebec's independence is not only desirable, but also inevitable. Micone remains convinced of this even after the racism inherent in Quebec Premier Jacques Parizeau's post 1995 referendum comment that "the Quebec nation had been defeated by money and the ethnic vote."

Marco Micone's francophile sympathies were clearly expressed in his poem-manifesto entitled "Speak What" (1993), inspired on one hand by the arrogant and at once disparaging sentiment ascribed to anglophone Canadians towards their French-speaking counterparts, and on the other by the poem by the Quebec sovereignist poet Michelle Lalonde entitled "Speak White." In "Speak What" Micone calls upon the various ethnic minorities which comprise Quebec to join forces with "old-stock" francophone Quebeckers, not merely for the survival, but clearly, for the future development of a French-speaking Quebec. If only Jacques Parizeau could be convinced of this!

A more personal and intimate tone is assumed by Micone in his existential memoir *Le figuier enchanté* (The

Magic Fig Tree) which appeared in 1992. As the title suggests, this volume describes childhood memories of growing up in his native Montelongo, a small village in the Appennine Mountains. The story, an interesting literary effort as memoirs go, is intended more so for the author's own delight. It manages to displace the author from his usually heavily-laden didactic and ideological production. The remembrance of the land of origin as myth prevalent in the first part of the book has brought about an artistic enrichment in Micone's literary *imaginaire,* and one cannot help but be pleased. However, in the latter part of the book Micone is unable to avoid the same pitfalls as in his theatre where he describes his arrival and integration into Quebec society.

Mary Melfi: Poetry and Prose

The sense of alienation experienced by immigrant women is one of the principal motifs in the work of many Italian Canadian authors. The dialectical rapport between the sexes and the complex *problématique,* which characterize it, is also the focal point in the work of Mary Melfi, born in Italy in 1951 and brought to Canada at the age of six.

Shy and introverted by nature, Melfi finds in the written word the ideal means to express her rage and her impotence as a woman and as the daughter of poor immigrants. It is the fact of belonging to a lower socio-economic class that Melfi sees as a handicap that prevents her full expression as a woman. In the small bourgeois Italian Canadian milieu the woman still plays a static, traditional role. She must be submissive, and possibly pretty, or at least elegant. She must play the part of conciliator, of mother, "of the Virgin, or at least of goddess of smiles, of beauty queen."[39] The result is that Melfi has greatly enriched the discourse on gender relations and the sexual, social, existential, and economic components these imply.

During her university years in the 1970s (at Loyola College and then at McGill University), Melfi found an outlet in feminism. She learned not to remain invisible any longer or merely a cheerleader to male success and superiority. She rebelled against her parents and the Italian

Canadian environment which still perpetuated the myth of male superiority. She criticized and condemned the male's chauvinistic and condescending attitudes. She is convinced, instead, that in Western post-industrial urban society such as urban Canada the relationship between men and women must be that of equals. There is no longer any need for physically strong men who order women around. Rather, according to Melfi, what society needs is men who are ready to have a dialogue and be equal partners with women.

The need for individual freedom as a woman and the desire to distance herself from her social condition as the daughter of blue-collar working people — because for her poverty is a calamity — have resulted in the fact that Mary Melfi as writer at first broke ties with her peasant Italian cultural heritage. She saw herself as a person who did not quite belong to any group; she considered herself simply Canadian. More recently, however, her attitude has become more nuanced, and the Italian dimension in her has started to play a role in her artistic *imaginaire.*

Convinced that one's attitudes and way of life are determined by social class instead of ethnic origin, Melfi did not at first pay much attention to her *italianità* in her work. Italy was no longer her country and Italian was no longer her language. Thus, she did not consider herself Italian Canadian, but simply Canadian, or better still, North American. She had lost her allegiance to Italy, even if she maintained some sentimental ties with the town where she was born. During a trip to Italy as a young university graduate she could not say she felt Italian. She simply saw herself as another tourist visiting cities in a country that even her parents could not recognize since they had always lived in the countryside.

The choice to adopt Canada incites Melfi to claim the right to belong, but as an *allophone* this request is denied her by the notion of the "two founding peoples." Melfi refuses to be labeled as belonging to *les autres* (the others). Unable or unwilling to intervene in the public debate on the Canadian identity because of her shy and introverted nature, Melfi channels her aggressiveness into a poetic language that is explosive, surreal, and ironic. This tendency is wrought from her fondness for the French surrealists and for Dylan Thomas, Ezra Pound, and e. e. cummings. Her preferences are manifested in her first collection of poems, *The Dance, the Cage, and the Horse* published in Montreal in 1976.

The rawness, if not the cruelty, of the images *à la Rabelais* also characterized her second volume, *A Queen Is Holding a Mummified Cat,* published by Guernica in 1982. The following year the same publisher printed *A Bride in Three Acts,* her third collection, and 1986 saw the publication in Toronto of *A Dialogue with Masks,* her first volume of prose.

From Melfi's phantasmagorical imagination gush forth images of amazing force and symbolism. Her surrealism expresses a striking existential anxiety. Her metaphors remind one of Marcel Duchamp, as well as Renaissance painters such as Arcimboldo or Hieronymus Bosch. Mary Melfi's language of poetry and prose possesses a mannerist connotation, almost serpentine, which impresses upon the language of English Canadian literature some rare syntactic contortions. The unconscious suddenly exploding into fragments is the best way to describe Melfi's style. Like Molly Bloom in Joyce's *Ulysses* or Lady Chatterley in the D.H. Lawrence novel, Melfi's technique is akin to the stream of consciousness whereby the character lives and sees herself living with a lucidity which borders on clairvoyance and madness. Her writings are the expression of an unstable balance between appearance and hallucination.

Her condition as woman, as an object and as a subject acting upon man, reaches the crisis point in the dynamics of sex, as several chapters of her novel *A Dialogue with Masks* abundantly reveal. Allegorical language with ironical twists is the only shield that, as a woman, Mary Melfi seems to possess to defend herself against the condescension and the oppressiveness of the male; or, as a citizen, against a country which refuses her the right to fully belong. Her collection of poems entitled *The Oh Canada Poems,* which appeared in Brandon, Manitoba, in 1986, attest to this. Her feminist discourse persists in works such as the play *Sex Therapy: A Black Comedy,* and in *Office Politics,* a soon to be published collection of poems. More recently, Mary Melfi has undertaken to discuss her condition as an "ethnic" artist. The novel *Infertility Rites,* published by Guernica in 1992, is her most complex work so far. In it she addresses questions such as the role of the artist, identity, motherhood, and the rediscovery of one's roots.

Given her shy but caustic nature, Melfi uses the pen like a hand grenade to blow up the apparent solidity of social conventions and the value system on which they are based. For instance, in the poem entitled "La demie vierge" in the collection *A Bride in Three Acts,* the marriage ceremony becomes a parody of modern life. Our civilization is reduced to a menu where love and death are just a game. The photographer's camera has a radioactive lens and romance itself becomes radioactive:

> The sun comes down one day
> in the shape of a man in a radioactive cape . . .
> He stares at you and you think his stares are worse
>   than bullets.
> You won't know what hit you for years . . .
> Following is so tragic.
> You believe tragedy is the only ending suitable
>   for a dull life . . .
> Radioactivity like romance . . .
> He puts your dreams in an envelope
> and seals it with a radioactive kiss.
> Your dreams are radioactive
> No one will touch them with a ten-foot pole
> So you place his cape on your shoulders.
> It's the only way to get out of the darkness.
>   Ad nauseam.

Even the bride and groom's rings are dangerous high-tech devices, mini-computers and satellites which record all the actions and the conversations of the newly weds. In "Act One," the bride smiles ambiguously to hide her apathy, and ends up seeing herself as an acrobat ready to "please the twentieth century."

The novel *A Dialogue with Masks* follows logically the marriage ceremony described in *A Bride in Three Act;* it is the relationship between husband and wife which becomes the focal point of Melfi's analysis. Instead of a simple dialogue, the discourse becomes a war of words between two nameless people, who, from Melfi's perspective, represent universal human archetypes.

What is striking in the exchange between husband and wife is the biting metaphorical language which reveals a succession of accusations and counter accusations. Sex, power, and death are the recurring themes, as well as an irreconcilable disparity in the point of view between male and female. Neither of the two characters is particularly likable, although the male is more detestable because he claims to believe in great ideals but in reality is just wearing a mask to hide his coarseness, as in this example: "Wrong, baby . . . Be nice. Agree with me . . . how many men can top my performance in bed?"

The female is somewhat more refined. It is through her words that Melfi reveals her own sensitivity as a woman and as an artist: "You do not know if I am beside you like a pair of artificial limbs you unhooked when you went to bed or if I am beside you like a white tuxedo you wore to a ball . . . But sex is a hell of a trick. It not only provides us with the vehicle to become a host of other people (good or bad), but it also ensures (in some cases) the creation of a new generation of pimps and prostitutes."

The metaphorical acrobatics become a scream for freedom when it is the existential condition of womanhood which hangs in the balance: "You want to reduce me to an extension of yourself, a piece you are missing. You want to rob me of what makes me what I am, to rob me of the very secrets of my femininity, of what makes me holy, in fact."

A similar combination of allegorical nastiness *(à la Hieronymus Bosch)* and black humour is present in Melfi's fourth collection of poems entitled *A Season in Beware* (1989). As usual, the focal point is the condition of woman in the dual role as wife and homemaker on one side, and career woman on the other. As expected, the portrait that has been drawn ends up being depressing.

Sin becomes a mechanical process and society is equated to a neon sign which promotes and advertises masochistic tendencies. Woman's only escape from her sentimental condition dominated by violence, alienation, and threats is humor of which the collection abounds. Only in the last few poems in the section entitled "Faith Healer" does one find a slightly less depressing tone as to what it is that binds man and woman: "Kiss me and my body might just wash itself of its need for you."

The emancipated woman who works and is successful, presented in "The Woman in Red," must be accountable to "the sea of butchery for the multitude of nine to fivers." Sitting on her throne, she watches the distorted figures of the wounded she has left behind in her rise to power, abandoned in the streets. She is aware, however, that a male will end up usurping her throne or that she will be replaced "with an acceptable doll, blond and anorexic, the model advertised in our post-industrial age." When she realizes that "she is nothing but a bouquet of wounds," she has no other recourse but to commit suicide.

In the soon to be published collection of poems *Office Politics,* Mary Melfi's social critique so predominant in *A Season in Beware* (1989), continues. Her target is the "office queens" who use their title as a weapon to allow the "amazonian forest of signs to work." She feels crushed by the jungle of computers; that type of work is dangerous for her mental health. To her work means becoming an extension of a machine: "I am the machine for my company / My company, the machine for God knows what." She sees herself as food for the computer that devours her mind. The office becomes a fighting field where the pen is mightier than the sword. The office manager practices emotional scalping. The employee feels that she is being drowned and she cries out for help in vain. "S.O.S. / I'm lost in someone else's country / wrapped in a flag of invisibility." Ms. Rosetta Stone, like a new Champollion of cybernetics, has to decipher computer language for her boss and keep feeding material to the company if she wants to keep her job.

> Ms. Rosetta Stone
> Will you hurry and come in here
> Please
> Give us a clue to what is going on
> Bring out another company manual
> This time tomorrow!
> Give us mining
> The last word Or else
> You're history.

Rather than live and work in a post-modern world of savage relationships ("Our enterprise cannot turn beastly / Against our neighbour / As it is already populated with beasts."), Rosetta Stone would like to become a mannequin in a store or a statue in a church. The alienation that she feels prevents her from being a full human being and a loving mother.

> Every night she tells her children lies about
> unconditional love
> They don't bother to listen
> Her heart is an empty space
> The doctors can't fix her.

What can Rosetta do when she discovers that her revolt against the system is doomed to fail? This is the question that Mary Melfi asks herself at the end of *Office Politics*.

> Revolution is messy . . .
> Better to shop for forgiveness than to plant
>   phantom bombs . . .
> I take my Prozac — instant religion —
> And sail through life
> While the rich shop for sailboats
> I shop for answers.

She smiles and, in order to protect herself, she wears a contagious virus with pride. She wants to be treated with dignity, but receives instead scorn. Nobody loves her and in order to avenge herself she would like to take the computer cable:

> Twist it around the neck
> Of our office tower
> That sick giant . . .
> And sometimes I want to twist the cable around
>   my own neck
> I also want my soul back.

Rather than commit suicide like the "The Woman in Red" or "Office Queen," the female character in the volume rediscovers that there are medicinal properties in the familiar. She allows her man to wrap himself around the circle of her needs and, thus, obtains "Form and content to this ghostly thing / which responds to my name." She can then float towards the divine and be satisfied with "prisons" that constitute the relation between two persons.

> There is safety in prisons
> My mate imprisons my timidity
> Such delight in being his victim
> In his grasp . . .
> My mate, my faith healer, my body tamer squeezes me
>   a little
> And a gorgeous perfume is emitted (household magic)
> Its sweetness poisons my sense of reality
> Sweetens up the everyday
> Suddenly I'm forgiven for my bad taste
> Being average — an ancestral sin.

She accepts most of all that in our cold, cruel world happiness should be sought in small, imperfect, short-lived doses, and can be found in things such as a glance, a conversation, and especially charity.

> Let's begin a wedding ceremony
> Between freedom and bondage
> Between plant and animal substance
> Let's abide by the rules of the dictator: togetherness
> I deliver myself to its openings
> My heart takes a quantum leap (better buckle up).

With her new wings she is able to conceive with her thoughts a little niche of the universe, to find a cord hanging from the heavens, imagination; and to fly beyond the solar system, and from far away wish "charity for the wicked above all else." This is a new message of hope in Mary Melfi's production (so much the better!) because in her poetry before *Office Politics* human life was nothing but a nightmare.

The novel *Infertility Rites* is Mary Melfi's best work in prose so far. The drama unfolds around the trials that an Italian Canadian painter Nina Di Fiore must overcome before she is able to bring her pregnancy to term. At first, she lives only for the sake of her art. Later on, married and in her thirties, her "biological destiny" begins to get the better of her. She feels irresistibly attracted to the traditional values of her childhood, particularly motherhood. In addition, she admits that even as an artist she feels inspired by the "grotesque and surreal images of children."

Daniel, her typical Anglo-Saxon Protestant husband, laughs at her sudden desire to have children, lashes out at her with professorial irony, and accuses her of being obsessed by her Italian origin. The rift between Daniel and Nina may be caused by their different ethnic origins, but it is exacerbated by the fact that he as a man and she as a woman think differently. Melfi effectively combines Nina's cultural alienation as an Italian Canadian, and her existential crisis as a woman when she, on two occasions, fails to bring her pregnancy to term.

Nina Di Fiore is living in a cultural and existential limbo, like a great number of Italian Canadian women of the second and third generations. On the one hand, as an artist she imitates and envies the bourgeois English Canadian childless feminist and career women; on the other, as an Italian Canadian woman, she is attracted to the model of the traditional woman as mother embodied by Dora, her happily pregnant nineteen-year-old cousin, the ideal daughter whom Nina's mother could only dream of having.

Nina's angst derives from her inability to feel fully integrated into Canadian culture and by her refusal (at first, and because of biological unfeasibility later) to be the traditional "Italian mother." Each miscarriage is minutely described, as are the psychological repercussions on Nina. After each miscarriage, she sinks ever deeper in anxiety and depression. It is in circumstances such as these that the traditional values of her Italian origin, and above all her Catholic religion, come to the fore and rescue her.

Black humour, so typical in Mary Melfi's artistic world, surfaces when the topic of motherhood is discussed between Nina and Daniel. When he first learns about his wife's wish to have a child, he reacts violently. But once he has accepted the idea of becoming a father, he blames his wife for her infertility. Nina fears being abandoned because of her inability to have the child that her husband now so desperately desires. Nina's biological infertility becomes yet another reason for their frequent quarrels and might even cause their breakup.

The search for maternity acquires several layers: psychological, social, sexual, and medical. Each of these layers is examined in such minute detail that at times they resemble studies in sociology, feminist ideology, or medical prognoses. It might have been *melius deficere quam abundare,* but Melfi seems to fear that Nina's spasmodic search for maternity and the troubles she confronts might seem suspect if they were not exhaustively explained. As such, the reader learns about the effects on the fetus when, for example, a woman ingests an aspirin or a cup of tea, and especially if she undergoes a test for amniocentesis.

Nina is literally horrified by the thought of giving birth to a physically handicapped or mentally retarded child. Nevertheless, her vocation as a mother helps her to overcome this fear and she declares herself ready to accept the newborn whatever its condition. Significantly, *Infertility Rites* ends with the mother welcoming the unborn child through an imaginary dialogue with it.

Mary Melfi's talent as a fabulatrix is revealed in the novella *Ubu, the Witch Who Would Be Rich.* Ubu is a fascinating and original fairy tale. In much children's literature the split between good and evil is always clear, and clearly good always triumphs over evil at the end. But in Mary Melfi's novella, this is not the case. The main character, Ubu is a precocious but poor ten-year-old country girl from Newfoundland who decides she must improve her family's lot. Thus, she decides to take courses by correspondence at the Royal Witch Academy. The Agency of Well Being Witches obliges all those who have acquired special powers to use them not for personal gain but to help others.

Ubu's parents end up losing their farm, and Ubu winds up in the children's ghetto in the city. In her new environment, thanks to her talent, Ubu quickly becomes everyone's favorite baby-sitter. But soon Ubu realizes that she is being exploited. She decides, as a result, to become rich. But how and when should she do it? She invents the philosopher's stone which can turn any metal into gold. But there is a price to pay for this breach of witchly protocol. Ubu must quit the Agency of Well Being Witches and join the Wicked Witches Agency. Will the virtuous Ubu end up accepting the offer made to her by Yfel, a wicked witch whose life slogan is "Hello! Be as mean as your heart desires"? Ubu considers her options and finds justification in her thirst for wealth by thinking about what Cinderella had tried to do and become. Cinderella clearly appears to Ubu as a criminal par excellence. Easy to guess how the story will end.

Ubu is a marvelous story; it is easy to draw parallels between it and a classic of children's literature, Carlo Collodi's *Le Avventure di Pinocchio.* Pinocchio the puppet and Ubu the rich witch are not pleasant characters; but they remain paradigms of the deep and indelible impulses of human nature. Pinocchio's and Ubu's experiences are steps towards an awareness of a world where good and evil confront each other and coexist. It is in this grey area, which obliges us as readers to investigate the dark side of human behaviour, that we find the wisdom of the likes of Collodi and Melfi. *Ubu, the Witch Who Would Be Rich* is a story which makes us laugh, but also makes us think. I am not overstating things when I say that it is a book for children which deserves attention, not just in Canada but throughout world. Because of the quality and abundance of her artistic production — poetry, prose and theatre, Mary Melfi is certainly one of the most interesting voices on the subject of women's issues in English-language Canadian literature.

Lisa Carducci's *Héliotropes*

Born in Montreal in 1943, Lisa Carducci is an interesting example of a third generation Canadian who felt the need to rediscover her Italian roots after undergoing the process of acculturation to the French-speaking majority in Quebec. Proof of this need is found in her intense activity as a journalist in Italian for the Montreal weekly *Il Cittadino canadese,* and in her collection of poems published in Italian under the title *L'ultima fede* (The Last Faith) in 1990. For the last several years Carducci has been contributing to *Il Cittadino canadese* from China, where she seems to have found yet a third adopted country.

Carducci is essentially a French-language writer. For this reason her use of Italian acquires a particular importance. Her first collection of poetry was entitled *Héliotropes.* The formally experimental qualities of this work resemble concrete poetry or even calligrammes, a sign that Carducci, a teacher by profession, followed very closely and participated in the renewal of the aesthetics of Quebecois poetry after the decline of Quebec nationalism in the early 1980s — a nationalism which had favoured political engagement and realism.

Another important motif in the work of Carducci, as exemplified in her collection *Nouvelles en couleurs* published in Montreal in 1985, is the manner in which she analyses human relations, especially between a man and a woman. Marital fidelity, abortion, the latent incest of a father for his murdered daughter, the nonfulfillment of a man's obligations towards his wife and his daughter whom he meets on a train: these are the topics of the four short stories which comprise the volume. *Nouvelles en couleurs* is good reading, without being exceptional, written in a colloquial language and a traditional narrative style.

A surprising aspect of Carducci's career as a writer is her reappropriation, after her experimental phase, of the Italian language as well as the immigrant motif. After visiting the country of her ancestors, she rediscovers a part of herself and writes poems like "Viaggio in Molise" and "Le coeur du Molise." Although she was born in Canada, Carducci feels the need for a physical and spiritual unification with the perceived reality of the ancestral land. In *L'ultima fede* Carducci aspires to a psychic balance that only an expression of the complexity of the phenomenology of love can provide. *L'ultima fede* is structured in episodes, somewhat resembling the typical Petrarchian *canzoniere,* a collection of love poems. In Carducci's collections we read about a man and a woman falling in love, enjoying love both spiritually and physically, then breaking up. This is followed by an all-consuming grief brought on by the memory of passionate moments, and finally there is despair brought about by love which is forever lost. The phenomenology of love in Carducci's *L'ultima fede* has traits which remind us of both the bride's lament of love in the Bible's Song of Songs, and the theory of spirits in the medieval Stil Novo school of poetry. As in Guido Cavalcanti's or even the young Dante's poetry, the spirits of love invade the eyes, the body and the mind of the object of love. Thus, reciprocity between the lover and the loved is established. A third element present in Carducci's collection of poems, which attaches her to the centuries-old Petrarchian tradition, is the meditation on past joy and the desperate remembrance of the lonely lover. This clearly suggests that there are natural constants in the process of falling in love which transcend time, and all lovers discover for themselves the joy, the pain, and the uncertainty of human emotions. The only other reality that allows Carducci to obtain, albeit momentarily, a physical and spiritual equilibrium are the hills that gave birth to her ancestors and which she physically rediscovers:

> When in the silence of the morning . . . you will remember the migration, when you will cry out for the desire of taking root in this country, when emptiness will invade your body with nostalgia, then, with mixed emotion, you will know the true heart of your land.

Vittorio Rossi's *Love and Other Games*

The son of immigrant workers from southern Italy, the Montreal-born Vittorio Rossi is an emerging voice in Canadian English-language theatre. To Montreal theatre lovers, however, Rossi is already well-known as the author of such plays as *The Chain, Scarpone,* and *The Last Adam.*

Vittorio Rossi, who holds a Bachelor's degree in drama from Concordia University, uses English as his main language of expression and creation, though he speaks relatively fluent Italian. In 1986 and 1987 he won top prize at the Quebec Drama Festival for his one-act plays *Little Blood Brother* and *Backstreets,* recently re-staged in Toronto. Since 1987 his main occupation has been to write for the theatre. March 1995 saw the premiere at Montreal's Centaur Theatre of Rossi's most recent play entitled *Love and Other Games.*

In addition to being a playwright, Vittorio Rossi has also done some acting, and has appeared in the C.B.C. television series *Urban Angels* in the role of Dino Marrone, and in such films as *Day One, Malarek,* and *Canvas.* "Acting is very physical work for which you have to be in good physical condition," says Rossi. "That's why I jog and cycle."

In the fall of 1988 Centaur Theatre staged Rossi's *The Chain,* which won Rossi critical attention and some popular acclaim. It also earned him comparisons to renowned Montreal playwrights David Fennario and Michel Tremblay for the manner in which his writing reveals a clear understanding of time and space, and how it realistically recreates contemporary Montreal social reality. *The Chain* was subsequently read at New York's Circle Repertory Company.

The Chain recounts the relationship between a father, Tullio Testa — an Italian immigrant just retired from his job as a gardener for the rich in plush Westmount — and his two sons, Massimo and Joe. In a series of dialogues which take place in the back yard and the garden of their working class, Ville Emard house, the father, in typical immigrant fashion, highlights the many sacrifices he made and the obstacles he had to overcome. He makes frequent reference to the difficult living conditions in both the old and new country. His children, born and raised in Canada in an urban environment, pursue different values and don't seem to appreciate the hardships and humiliations endured by their father. From this mutual misunderstanding arises the conflict between the three characters. Not unlike other Italian Canadian writers, Vittorio Rossi underlines the inevitable conflict of two clashing realities. In April 1989 *The Chain* was staged at the National Arts Center in Ottawa.

The topics treated in Vittorio Rossi's plays are not necessarily the product of his personal experience. The identity crisis suffered by second generation Italian Canadians or the conflicts between parents and children are simply in his case artistic archetypes. "My father," Rossi clarifies, "is a man with a broad viewpoint who accepts change. Even though he encouraged his children to speak Italian at home, for us being raised in Canada, it is much more natural and spontaneous to speak English. I am very attached to my family and I feel very much at ease in the family environment. Getting together with my parents for Sunday lunch is not a burden in the least — it's a pleasure."

In 1989, Dawson College staged Rossi's *In Pursuit of a Cow.* Rossi's experience as a shoe salesman for six years inspired him to write *Scarpone,* staged by Centaur in 1990, which received rave reviews and played to packed houses. In 1989 Maurice Podbrey, Centaur's artistic director, recognizing Rossi's undeniable talent, appointed him Centaur's writer-in-residence. The same recognition was bestowed on Rossi the following year by Concordia University.

In *The Last Adam,* staged by Centaur in 1994, Rossi delves into the secrets of an Italian Canadian Montreal family, where conflict exists not just between father and sons (as in *The Chain*), but also between husband and wife, and brothers and sisters. In the first act of the two-act play the main character, Sal, tries to shed his image as a loser by trying to talk his older brother and his cousin into starting up a fur-importing business. Sal is equally disturbed by his self-perception as an uprooted person — a stranger in the city where he was born and where speaking English is becoming a liability.

The idea for *The Last Adam* came to Vittorio Rossi during the summer of 1990 in the midst of the Oka Crisis, the confrontation between Natives and the Quebec government. Rossi felt quite disturbed by the government's reaction to the Native people's protest. Moreover, seeing that many Quebecois reacted to the English-speaking Mohawks by pelting them with stones, as they drove away to safety, made him feel personally attacked and led him to ask himself if there is room in today's Quebec for "others." The tirade against the French-speaking waiter in the early part of the play is Rossi's reaction to the ethnocentrism and the prejudice which he perceives in nationalist Quebecois public opinion. This element of social criticism, presented in the first act, constitutes an important aspect of *The Last Adam*.

One of the strengths of the play is the reproduction of the sounds of lively, colloquial dialogue in which four-letter words abound, a language which expresses the characters' ethnicity and socio-economic status. One could describe it as *Italianese* — a mixture of different Italian dialects, standard Italian, French, and English — the slang that the majority of first generation Italians living in Montreal actually speak.

It is difficult to classify *The Last Adam,* for the play fuses traditional theatrical genres. From the initial lighthearted twists typical of a comedy, Rossi leads the spectators to the final anguished ending typical of a tragedy. Perhaps melodrama (without any derogatory connotation) is the best way to define the play. Only in this category can the plot acquire meaning and a plausible classification.

Moreover, one has the feeling that *The Last Adam* is the junction of two different plays. This incongruity constitutes its dramatic flaw. Another bothersome element of the play are Sal's constant references to his criminal connections (as if every Italian Canadian, because of his ethnic background, must necessarily have links to the Mafia), and the quasi-mythical — and consequently grotesque — dimension that family unity plays in the value system of Canadians of Italian origin.

My suspicion (and the audience's laughter and reactions at the première seemed to confirm it) is that Vittorio Rossi fashioned in *The Last Adam* a product which an English-speaking audience would find appetizing, especially in the first act, because of the frequent use of stereotypical clichés — a practice which I hope Rossi will refrain from in the future, otherwise his undeniable artistic talent will be reduced, little by little, to folklore, to an ethnic product which makes some people laugh, but which does not count for much.

Love and Other Games is Vittorio Rossi's latest and best work yet! It is characterized by lively language, an intelligent mix of the comical and the tragic, and a psychological incisiveness not commonly seen. It is convincing in the way the search for love realigns the relationship between four couples. The play, reminiscent of Pirandello's *Six Characters in Search of an Author,* could well be retitled *Eight Characters in Search of Love . . . in a Piano Bar.*

Indeed, a piano bar is where labyrinthine manifestations of passion take place over the course of four seasons.

Jimmy, the Irish widower and owner of the piano bar, lives with the painful memory of his wife who died three years before. Nicole, a French-Canadian editor, introduces him to Rosie, a mature woman and a teacher who is of Italian Canadian background. After some hesitations Jimmy and Rosie succeed in establishing a relationship. Things prove more trying for Nicole, and equally so for Fernie and his on-again-off-again English girlfriend Susie.

Love and Other Games deals with traditional themes: the difficulty of discovering one's true self and the nature of love. These, of course, are universal themes with illustrious antecedents, but Rossi's original presentation gives them a certain degree of freshness and novelty. The social context and the spatial/temporal coordinates trace a precise portrait of modern-day Montreal. Frequent reference is made, for instance, to Ville-Emard, the Montreal suburb where Rossi was born and raised.

Vittorio Rossi's message in *Love and Other Games* is fundamentally optimistic. There can be love between fellow human beings, but each one of us must find the key to it all alone. In order to attain love we must avoid mathematical equations, as well as abstract schemes, since our behaviour obeys mysterious laws, especially when what is at stake is romance, the inescapable human mystery par excellence. Our existence, Rossi suggests in the play, is an equation between our virgin emotional potential and the obstacles which prevent us from growing, such as cynical calculation and unscrupulousness. It becomes necessary, therefore, to discover the reasons for our actions, reasons which are understood at the instinctive level, but which are to be expressed by means of the right words.

Fundamental, from an ontological point of view in *Love and Other Games* is the role of Fernie. The character has great difficulty completing his sentences. He has greater ease "seeing" words than actually hearing them, yet he cannot seem to find the verbal equivalents when he speaks. He lives on the borderline between two worlds: the everyday world dominated by selfishness, incomprehension, non-communication, and pain; and the "other" world which he carries within himself and which he expresses through his music. In this other world, "there is no pain; all the thoughts are clouds of happiness; no one has a gun to his head; ears cannot hear lies." These are the words to the song Fernie sings towards the end of the play. Ironically, the character who had the greatest difficulty communicating, eloquently reveals the author's message: our world would be a better place if only love could triumph. It would be good, indeed, but it would mean changing human nature.

The language in *Love and Other Games* is colloquial, as one would expect in a play by Rossi. However, notwithstanding the laughter resulting from puns and contextual references, the dialogue in *Love and Other Games* is infused with metaphorical references and existential considerations. Rossi attains an ontological dimension which was not as present in his previous works.

Nino Ricci's *Lives of the Saints* and After

Among contemporary English Canadian writers of Italian descent, Nino Ricci is the best known. He burst onto the literary scene in 1991, after winning the Francesco Giuseppe Bressani Award as well as the Governor General's Award, Canada's highest honor, for his first novel *Lives of the Saints* (1991). Snubbed by prospective publishers at first, the novel (which had been written as a Master's thesis in creative writing at Concordia University) found its way back into the hands of Garry Geddes, Ricci's thesis advisor, who printed it through his publishing house. The novel was immediately successful: after just one week, a second edition was issued. The novel remained on the best seller's list for several months and has been translated into seven languages, including French and Italian. Ricci's meteoric rise to fame was unbelievable even to him. He says: "It felt like a joke, like an elaborate conspiracy to humiliate me in some way. I thought somebody would come along at some point and snatch it all away."[40]

Nino Ricci, the fourth of six children, was born in 1959 in the town of Leamington in southern Ontario. His parents emigrated from the province of Isernia in south central Italy and arrived in Canada in 1954, where they worked as vegetable growers. "When I was young," says Ricci, "I had a lot of fantasies about what I would do when I was old, and most of them involved fame and fortune, so any profession which would allow for that was an acceptable one."[41]

In his youth, Ricci had wanted to become a hockey player or an actor, but the first career he seriously considered was that of priest. He gave that up in the fifth grade, however, when he gained a reputation for writing stories.

Raised in a tightly-knit family environment which perpetuated the peasant mentality left behind in the home village of Villa Casale, Ricci, like many other second generation Canadian writers, had to come to terms with the conflictual nature of his life at home and life outside. Life at home with family, relatives, and friends focused around the memories of the land of origin and on a patriarchal system of values. Outside, in the streets of Leamington, life evolved around a different language and a different set of values. "Entering school was like entering a different world. There was in my mind a definite split between what went on at home and what went on in the rest of the world. I often lived through a sense of being a charlatan at school. I felt that my whole job there was to pretend that I was not what I was when I went home."[42]

Like any child, Ricci wanted to be accepted, to be like the other children, to assimilate. But his sense of being different made it impossible for him to distinguish between his Italian roots and his condition as the son of working-class immigrants. Being an immigrant and being

Italian remained closely associated in Ricci's mind during his childhood and teen-age years.

The feeling, during his youth, of being suspended between two irreconcilable realities made Ricci feel alienated, almost inferior; but, with the passing of time, this feeling became the source of his inspiration. The magical realism which characterizes his first two novels — particularly *Lives of the Saints* (1991), as well as *In a Glass House* (1993) — owes much to Ricci's capacity to reconstruct the lifestyles of his ancestors filtered through the memory that had been kept of it by the Italians of Leamington. In the first novel the peasant culture, typical of a Molisan village like Villa Casale and transplanted onto Canadian territory as a result of immigration, is nostalgic and unable to overcome its sense of physical and mental dislocation. The reality in *Lives of the Saints* is atemporal: its concreteness is surrounded by a halo of unreality, all the while minutely described.

Nino Ricci's literary output is to an extent a result of his "split personality," not unlike that of many other Italian Canadian writers. It arises from the conflict between present-day urban Canada and private remembrances. Ricci attempts to combine his sophistication as an urbanite with the indelible burden of the heritage borne from the Italian peasant village mentality.

The sense of isolation and of non-belonging experienced by Ricci during his youth, thus, transformed itself over the years into the source of his artistic output. To recreate the elements of two very different worlds through the written word is the assignment that Ricci has taken on in his trilogy on the migration of the Innocente family. In recounting this Italian Canadian saga, Ricci demands the right to belong; something which the Anglo-Canadian literary establishment is not quite ready to grant Canadians of "other" origins.

"I think the very label 'ethnic' is so problematic, and I'm not the only one to feel this way. The origins of the term already give it a negative connotation because initially it meant pagan or heathen. It was a derogatory term for who was outside the real group. I don't think that average Italian Canadians think of themselves as ethnic. They think of themselves as who they are. It is only a label that is applied as soon as you become a marginal group within some other supposedly more dominant, more real culture which never calls itself ethnic, even though, of course, it would be. I mean Anglo-Saxon culture is no less ethnic than Italian or Ukrainian, but you don't see the CBC refer to their programming as ethnic, even though they have tended to be white, Anglo-Saxon . . . So the term normally has, in its connotation and in its denotation, the sense of a minority culture which is also, somehow, less important, less universal, less concerned with the entire society. I certainly don't think of myself writing that way. I don't think of writing for an ethnic community. I don't think of writing as a representative of an ethnic community. Therefore, the term has meaning for me only as a convenience, as a way of saying, 'This guy was born of Italian parents.' But that's just one fact among many others."[43] Nevertheless, thanks to the universality of the subject and to the talent of authors such as Nino Ricci, contemporary Canadian literature being produced by writers of Italian ancestry is gaining acceptance (albeit, slowly), as is demonstrated by the increasingly positive reactions by the mainstream Canadian press. This newly acquired legitimacy is allowing Italian Canadian writers to stand as a concrete example of the validity of the concept of multiculturalism as a new and viable basis for a redefinition of the Canadian identity. It is causing many to call into question the French/English dichotomy which is still presented as the official expression of what it means to be Canadian and causing others to challenge the traditional artistic canons. In this process of legitimization, the role played by Nino Ricci, however involuntarily, has been and remains noteworthy, for no one dare challenge his "Canadianness."

In the novel *Lives of the Saints,* a semi-autobiographical story, Nino Ricci describes life in Valle del Sole in 1960, an imaginary town in the mountains of south central Italy. Not unlike real-life, the town exists almost entirely cut off from modern reality. The town's inhabitants live by a very traditional value system which mixes pagan myths and superstitions with an almost medieval form of Catholicism. Using a technique reminiscent of Gabriel Garcia Marquez, Ricci begins his account with the description of an event which plants the seed for the unfolding of the rest of the plot.

"If this story has a beginning, a moment at which a single gesture broke the surface of events like a stone thrown into the sea, the ripples cresting away endlessly, then that beginning occurred on a hot July day in the year

1960, in the village of Valle del Sole, when my mother was bitten by a snake."[44]

This is no ordinary snakebite. From that point on, the events which take place forever change the life of Cristina Innocente and her seven-year old son Vittorio, the narrator. As his family name implies, Vittorio is innocent as well as content — loved by both his grandfather (the town mayor), and by his mother (a white widow), whose husband had left her four years earlier when he had immigrated to Canada. To quell her desire for affection, Cristina commits adultery; and on the very same day that she has carnal relations with her lover, she is bitten by a snake. Vittorio, who had caught a glimpse of a man leaving the scene, refuses to believe that her mother could love a man other than his father.

The townsfolk do not see things in quite the same way. Though they have few clues, they uncover the truth; for why else would Cristina have been bitten by a snake! For the town's "wise old women," among whom pagan beliefs are still quite strong, being bitten by a snake has a symbolic significance and a clear sexual connotation. The "evil tongues" get their way and ruin Cristina's reputation, this despite or perhaps because of her independent nature and her strong character which will not allow her to be conditioned by her environment.

For the townsfolk, the snakebite gives rise to the *malocchio* (evil-eye), an ancient and powerful pagan belief similar to *fatum*, which Christian religion cannot explain. The snakebite suffered by Cristina is irrefutable proof for her fellow townsfolk that she is cursed. She, on the other hand, has the effrontery of not admitting the truth. Cristina refuses an ointment for the bite given her by one of the "wise women," preferring instead to be taken to the hospital.

For the most part, the book describes the battle Cristina wages in her refusal to conform to the beliefs and superstitions of the village. Nevertheless, the villagers cross themselves whenever they go by her house, and Vittorio's schoolmates beat him up; even the grandfather begins to lose his authority as mayor. These events, however, do not set the stage for the novel's tragic conclusion when the pregnant mother and son decide to leave Villa del Sole to join the father in Canada. During the crossing of the Atlantic, Cristina gives birth to a baby girl whom she names Margherita. The delivery, however, has tragic consequences.

Ricci's second novel, *In a Glass House,* continues the saga with Vittorio and his little sister Margherita reunited with the father in the little farming town of Mersea in Southern Ontario. The meeting between father and son is overshadowed by the tragic death of the mother, and even more so by the shame Mario Innocente feels over the birth of the little girl, obvious proof of his wife's infidelity. Within the confines of Mersea's little Italian community, honor, and fidelity remain sacrosanct values. It is only logical, therefore, that having been cuckolded, the father can only feel hostility towards his dead wife's daughter. The neighbors try to help, but there is no happiness nor love in the Innocente household.

The leitmotif of Ricci's second novel is the alienation and the lack of communication between father and son. "There seemed to be no language between the two of us that was not somehow tinged by misunderstanding." Another main theme is emotional dislocation as expressed by Vittorio, who very much like the author, must come to terms with two different realities. Through Vittorio, Ricci also expresses the main theme of *In a Glass House,* which is the migration of identity.

Vittorio suffers from an incurable illness, "a narrow islanded gloom," which permeates his entire being as well as his relationship with the outside world. Upon his arrival in Mersea he is struck by the linear, almost Euclidean, topography of the landscape. This is in sharp contrast to the mountainous terrain he left behind in Valle del Sole.

Relations with other people are difficult, as well, in the new land. The father no longer sleeps in his bedroom, but in the basement next to the furnace. He leaves Vittorio to take care of his little sister, and ostracizes the little girl in much the same way as his wife had been ostracized by the townsfolk in Italy. The latent aggressiveness, even hatred, that Mario feels towards Margherita comes to a head when he brutally beats her as she tries to save the family dog — the only living being to which she had become attached, and which Mario shoots dead with a rifle. After this violent incident, the girl goes to live with the Amhersts, the parents of a classmate, who decide to adopt her.

Vittorio, too, faces a multitude of problems. Inevitably, a difficult childhood results in a problematic adolescence and an introverted adult life without any happiness. Sex, drugs, religion, and psychotherapy are some of the phases the character must go through before he garners the courage to leave to become an English teacher in Nigeria. Even the African experience recounted in the novel by means of a series of letters between father and son written in a rudimentary, broken language (especially the father's) does not resolve the misunderstandings between them, nor do they enable Vittorio to acquire a feeling of belonging. As he is about to renew his teaching contract, Vittorio is informed that his father has drowned.

The saga of the Innocente family continues in the third volume. Only then will we know if from the magical realism of *Lives of the Saints* to the *bildungsroman* of *In a Glass House* Nino Ricci has been capable of fashioning a tale where one's origins, ability to plant roots in a new land, integration and existential search, will be convincingly amalgamated to produce a saga where Italy and Canada, countryside and city, human relations and generation conflicts, search for identity and belonging come together and become the identity cards of the Italian Canadians, who from voiceless people will be elevated to universal human archetypes.

Part III
The Cinema of the Italian Canadians

The Films of Paul Tana

Paul Tana is a name that matters in contemporary French-language Canadian cinema.[45] What makes Paul Tana particular and interesting is the fact that he affixes an Italian sensitivity to the analysis of the society in which he lives. Tana's films demonstrate that one can be both an artist and express Quebec's urban reality, particularly Montreal, differently than has been traditionally done by other Quebec film-makers. It is the precariousness of this cosmopolitan reality, the co-existence of differences, that constitute this film-maker's source of inspiration rather than the search for the person's roots in the land. This marks a departure in Quebecois cinematographic culture. The themes that Tana addresses are present in many other countries, not just Canada. The question of otherness has become a worldwide concern. By focusing on the Montreal migrant reality, Paul Tana raises the very complex question of how to establish a balance between an artist's longing for his roots and his need to open up to a worldwide audience. This is probably the main characteristic of Paul Tana's concerns as an artist and as a film-maker.

The question of otherness is of crucial importance in present-day urban Quebec. By focusing on the Italian presence in this predominantly French-speaking society, he questions the ethnocentric perception of what it means to be a Quebecois. He demonstrates that otherness, an inescapable fact in the Montreal of today, has deep roots going as far back as New France. This is the thematic novelty of Tana's works, for he challenges the accepted notions of belonging. To analyze his films means to reflect on a new way of looking at identity and how different contributions can enrich society. Tana's films demonstrate how the different ethnic components of Montreal need to find a new *modus vivendi et operandi* in order that tolerance and mutual respect become accepted standards and the basis of a new collective awareness. In analyzing Tana's films, therefore, my goal is certainly to discuss their themes, but also to extrapolate and arrive at *un discours de société.*

Tana's opus spans more than twenty years of cinematic effort: *Les Étoiles et autres corps* (1973) — reaching the boundaries of the self; *Deux contes de la rue Berri: Pauline* and *Les gens heureux n'ont pas d'histoire* (1976) — a look at daily life; *Les Grands Enfants* (1979) — between precariousness and the search for identity; La Série Planètes — *Eight Portraits of Montreal* (1980), "Derrière la porte fermée/Oltre la porta chiusa," "3e Culture/Terza Cultura," "Les jeunes/I Giovani," "La presse de Montreal/La Stampa di Montreal," "La Fête/La Festa," "Le Retour/Il Ritorno," "Marriages/Matrimoni," "St-Léonard et après/St-Leonard e dopo;" *Caffè Italia, Montréal* (1985) — the story of three generations; *Le Marchand de jouets* (1989) — a casual encounter and the longing for passion; *La Sarrasine* (1992) — a Saracen woman among the maple trees; *La déroute (1998)* — the doom of a man's origins.

Two major thematic patterns are discernible so far in Tana's approach: the first is a penchant for an ontological discourse on cinema as an art form. This streak is to be found in *Les Étoiles et autres corps, Les Grands Enfants, Le Marchand de jouets,* and to a point also in *La déroute.* The character of Alex in *Les Étoiles et autres corps* questions the absurdity of being, the impossibility of knowing. Similarly, François and his friends in *Les Grands Enfants* face the precariousness of daily life, the lack of great ideals, the refusal to define themselves socially and accept *la petite vie* to the point of near vagrancy. Marianne and Charles in *Le Marchand de jouets,* as a result of their casual encounter on a train, behave as if they have been removed from reality and its spatial-temporal coordinates while playing games of seduction but longing for passion. Joe in *La déroute* questions the role images play in linking his existence as a well-to-do businessman and jealous father with the memory of his peasant origins.

The second thematic pattern brings to the fore a socio-historical dimension and the quest for identity. This is found particularly in *Les gens heureux n'ont pas d'historie,* La Série Planètes, *Caffè Italia, Montréal, La Sarrasine,* as well as *La déroute.* To an extent it also present in *Les Grands Enfants.* The characters of Nino in *Pauline,* Jeanne Rossi in *Les Grands Enfants,* Ninetta in *La Sarrasine,* and Joe Pagano, and actors Pierre Curzi, and Tony Nardi in *Caffè Italia, Montréal* — all question their own sense of belonging. Their remembrance of their homeland is expresses as a love-hate relationship and as a more or less self-aware desire to forge a new identity for themselves. Their search follows a dynamic logic and expresses itself in several stages. Nino, even on the verge of death, is still a deracinated Italian; he still lives in a mental ghetto strangled by his recollections. He resents Italy for obliging him to emigrate. The Italian-born Jeanne Rossi, who grew up in Montreal, embodies a complete almost nihilistic lack of self-awareness, for she feels neither Italian nor Canadian.

In *Caffè Italia, Montréal* Paul Tana expands the quest for identity by searching for the collective consciousness of the Italian community. Three generations confront one another while looking for a definition of their being. Often a character contradicts himself stressing both the need to preserve his Italian identity and the desire to be defined after many years spent living in Montreal as more than a simple immigrant. In *Caffè Italia, Montréal,* the director's objective is open and can lead to many solutions. This is contrary to what Tana has done in the past, for example, in his Série Planètes where Tana employed a didactic technique which supported the Parti Québécois government's policy of integration.

In *Caffè Italia, Montréal,* actor Pierre Curzi is not really concerned by the issue of the quest for *italianità*: he considers himself fully Quebecois. However, other people interviewed in the film do not exclude the possibility of going back to Italy. Actor Tony Nardi, for instance, is perceived as Italian by both English and French Canadians, and as Canadian by the Italians of the older generation still trapped in their self-excluding immigrant perception. Nardi himself cannot find the words to define who he really is. Past, present, and future intertwine and identity is still and open question. This is one of the merits of the film and corresponds to what Paul Tana himself must have felt while shooting it.

The discourse on identity unfortunately acquires once again a didactic dimension in *La Sarrasine.* In principle this feature film has a fictional plot, however, it was based upon a historical event which occurred at the beginning of the century in Montreal. In the film Giuseppe Moschella is a pseudonym for Giaccone, a tailor of Sicilian origin, who was condemned to hang for killing a French Canadian in a fight. Giuseppe Moschella becomes a fully integrated immigrant who has French Canadian friends like Alphonse Lamoureux, speaks good French, reads the French dailies, and is aware of what happens around him. He is a *néo-Québécois modèle,* as we would say today, honest, hardworking, who knows his place, but who ends up becoming an outlaw as a result of an ill-fated fight with Théo Lemieux. After the killing he once again becomes *l'étranger,* the foreigner, the outsider who must be punished in an exemplary manner by the authorities. Ninetta, Giuseppe's wife, follows a totally different path in her search for self-assertion. At the beginning of the film she is la sarrasine, who by means of a cathartic process (her husband's suicide and her refusal to obey his orders to go back to Sicily) acquires self-consciousness. She moves away from her traditional milieu and becomes the symbol of *enracinement* a "rerooting." This is where Tana's (and co-screenwriter Bruno Ramirez's) pedagogic intent, present throughout the film, becomes most evident and constitutes an artistic weakness of the film. The very complex and contradictory process of how one goes about acquiring a new identity is presented almost recipe-like.

In *La déroute,* Joe Pagano is an urban villager, a wealthy businessman within Montreal's well-integrated Italian community. He sees himself and is seen by others as an Italian Canadian, and therefore his legitimacy in belonging is not questioned. He still speaks a *français sale* (common street French). Joe Pagano's way of speaking is the mirror of his lack of formal education and his peasant origins, which manifest themselves in his superstitious beliefs and his attachment to traditional family values. Having made it in Canada, and living in comfort engender in him a form of extreme patriotism which push him to reject people who live on the economic and legal fringes of society such as Diego, the Dominican illegal immigrant who falls in love with his daughter Bennie.

In the film Bennie is open towards the Other. She is able to incorporate and accept ethnic difference by wanting to marry Diego, a photographer by profession but a fishmonger as a result of his illegal entry into Canada (a man who cannot get a steady job). After her father's death Bennie goes back to her Italian roots and finally accepts them as a component of her being. If Bennie is the most up-to-date expression of Tana's mental outlook, then we are presented with a complex, interesting, and multi-faceted view of contemporary Canadian social reality. Through Bennie, Tana questions the accepted notion by the so-called "two founding peoples" of what it means to be Canadian. Bennie as a character is richer than Ninetta because she does not constitute a pre-determined model of integration, nor is she a *Québécoise de souche.* What remains to be seen is whether the critics and public especially in Quebec will want to identify with the image Bennie personifies.

The two main thematic patterns present in Paul Tana's works, as has been suggested, show the importance that the quest for identity plays in Tana's films. By looking diachronically at his work, one can follow the different stages of the phenomenon of migration. With *La déroute* Tana says what he had to say. Will he be able to refashion himself and move on to deal with new themes? If Tana and Ramirez still pursue the quest for identity, they risk repeating themselves and becoming prisoners of the *problématique* of ethnicity. Tana has complained several times of being a victim of the wrong classification. The French-language critics have referred to him, depending on the purpose and occasion they wanted him to fit, as a full-fledged Quebecois, as an ethnic film-maker and as a neo-Quebecois. These different classifications imply a social and political discourse which is tacitly accepted and expressed by the French-speaking establishment. Journalists and academic critics use the same parlance, which presupposes a voluntary break between Quebec and the rest of Canada, even in cultural matters. English-language critics have defined Paul Tana as a full-fledged Canadian director, especially after the choice of *La Sarrasine* as the official Canadian entry at the 1992 Berlin Film Festival. Nevertheless, even in English Canada the danger of ethnic labeling endures. The fact remains that Paul Tana is either purposely claimed or unconsciously marginalized by both the anglophone and francophone critical establishment. Neither takes into account Paul Tana's self-perception and self-definition as artist, Montrealer and Italian.

Another danger that Tana faces is seeing his films defined as docufictions, or docudramas, which have an undeniable social historical interest, but which cannot be classified as genuine works of art. Tana has always claimed his legitimacy as an artist; he has always refused to be perceived as a simple "illustrator" who borders on the documentary and whose only goal is to describe the evolution of the Italian community. If Tana continues to be the defender of a politically correct message and a feel-good morality as is the case in *La Sarrasine* (his most ambitious work so far), he could become trapped in his own game and become a prisoner of his own ideological discourse. Didacticism is the danger that he must avoid.

The analysis of Paul Tana's film production, from the early 1970s to the mid 1990s, inevitably leads to a reflection on whether the act of creation ought to remain free of any ideological and political impositions and whether or not social constraints are inevitable. This raises an even more important question: the degree of freedom that both Quebec and Canadian society are willing to grant an artist. Must he necessarily defend a cause? Must he accept the dominant parameters when dealing with identity and ideology? Does he need only to corroborate them and become part of them? Or must the artist obey a moral imperative that obliges him to claim individual freedom which ends up marginalizing him? When the National

Film Board of Canada listed the films produced in 1992, it listed *La Sarrasine* as an "ethnic" film. One wonders if this was an honest mistake or a deliberate attempt to marginalize.

Enigmatico

*A Conversation with Patricia Fogliato
and David Mortin*

F.S. *Enigmatico* is a film about being a Canadian artist of Italian origin. Why did you choose the title *Enigmatico*?[46]

P.F. It came from Mary di Michele's poem "Enigmatico" in which she explains the image of her straddling the Atlantic with one foot in a village in the Abruzzi and the other in Toronto. That image really rang true for us and that is the reason why the film begins with that precise quotation.

D.M. It was a starting point. *Enigmatico* is a film about identity and somehow we had to say it at the outset. We needed to make it clear, and that image captured our attention. However, there is no definite conclusion in this search.

F.S. Allow me to use intellectual jargon. Can one classify your film as an "open work," as Umberto Eco would put it, and as post-modern criticism would go about defining it, in the sense . . .

D.M. . . . it is ambiguous . . .

F.S. . . . that the viewer will have to do some thinking of his own to understand what it means to be a Canadian artist of Italian origin? You do not provide a definite picture.

P.F. Exactly. We wanted the viewer to feel the emotions and the vibrations expressed by the people we interviewed without reaching a definite conclusion. Identity remains an open question.

F.S. Your editing of the images follows a circular pattern. You begin by showing the loss of one's homeland with the existential anguish this loss entails; then you move on to deal with the complex and difficult process of acculturation and split personality, and you end up proposing a new, widened awareness of what it means to belong to the Canadian reality. Is this a good line of reasoning?

D.M. Yes, this is how we structured the film. We felt that all the artists in Enigmatico had the experience of growing up with a set of three mental patterns: connection, disconnection and reconnection.

P.F. Each of the artists has grown up in an Italian family, but at one point each felt the need to rebel against its traditional value-system in order to accomplish full growth as a human being and as an artist. Connection is a synonym for innocence, purity, and wholeness which cannot last. Disconnection stands for the inevitable loss of a protective but, at the same time, stifling mind-set and social expectations. And reconnection implies both the existential quest and the expression of one's full potential as an artist, proud of one's specific ethnic background, but aware of the need to avoid a ghetto mentality.

F.S. How did you go about choosing the fifteen artists who appear in the film? Why did you pick an opera singer (Louis Quilico), a sculptor (Carmelo Arnoldin), playwrights (Marco Micone and Maristella Rocca), poets (Mary di Michele and Gianna Patriarca), novelists (Nino Ricci, Antonio D'Alfonso), a photographer (Vincenzo Pietropaolo), musicians (Quartetto Gelato), and a painter (Vincent Mancuso)?

D.M. We wanted a texture, different tones and approaches, different levels of visual, oral and aural dimensions. We had, from the very beginning, imagined words and images interweaving, becoming a tapestry.

P.F. We also wanted there to be a sense that all of these artists together are a community, but at the same time each of them is unique and each answers his/her search for identity in a different way. The universality of their message lies not in the fact that they belong to a specific ethnic group, the Italian one, but in their artistic vocation and quest. The questions they ask themselves are the same questions artists of whatever origin and everywhere in the world have to face and try to resolve.

D.M. We hope that anyone from whatever background can relate to what the artists we present on the screen are saying. The specifics may change for someone of, say, Jewish or Hungarian origin, but the essential spirit is the same. The desire and the quest are the same.

F.S. It is a process of migration and the goal to be attained is universal.

P.F. Exactly. We aimed to show a quest typical of all people and provided the context where to find one's identity. Some find it in their family and in the values they were raised with and either kept or rejected them. What is at stake is culture.

F.S. Nonetheless this culture has to be embedded in history, in the specifics that have shaped the traditions of Italians in Canada. It is not by accident that you chose my reading of the poem to Giovanni Caboto, which goes back to the Age of Discovery, and you end up presenting Arnoldin wanting to build a gigantic cathedral on Canadian soil at the end of the present millennium where people of all races can go and worship together.

D.M. Your poem to Giovanni Caboto represents the act of emigration and Caboto may be taken as the symbol of the first immigrant to Canada. As the film progresses, however, it is the process of growing up of the subsequent generations that becomes more important. That is why we are interested in letting your two sons, who are now the third generation, explain who they are, what they are inheriting from you — but also how they are being shaped by other social forces, especially in present-day Quebec. The body of the film is the aftermath of immigration and the struggle for a new identity, although, as you point out, it is embedded in history.

P.F. One element that stands out in *Enigmatico* is the drastic passage from a peasant to an urban reality and how it ends up being linked to the generation gap. The change that takes place in one generation is massive. The first generation was shaped by values of a rural, almost semi-feudal reality, whereas the subsequent generations are really the product of an urban environment. That produces a huge generation gap. I feel this gap in me.

D.M. This gap is well explained by the photographer Vincenzo Pietropaolo. He talks about his father carrying bricks and the very concrete way he relates to a city like Toronto. Vincenzo, on the other hand, stresses that he had to wait for two hours for the clouds to pass before he could take a picture of the same building. The difference is striking. Vincenzo's father toiled to build the city physically, whereas he is doing it symbolically. In your case the gap is somewhat blurred. Your wine-making at home is a trait of a rural tradition, but, being a university professor, you are a more sophisticated "urban villager."

F.S. I would like to link the generation gap to the gender bias that comes out so forcefully in Mary di Michele's and Gianna Patriarca's poetry and utterances. For them the conflict is really between civilizations, between peasantry and urbanity.

P.F. It was very important that differences between the male and female quests be brought out because they follow very diverging paths. In the static, patriarchal reality of first-generation Italian Canadian life, it is much more difficult for women to become self-assertive. There is a dimension of oppression they have to bear and react against. Their art is the means they use to free themselves. They are not victims because they manage to overcome the shortcomings imposed on them, but this truth must not be hidden.

F.S. I agree, but my feeling is that in the case of di Michele and especially of Patriarca the mistreatment she received by her father is heavy-handed. A different attitude towards Italian Canadian family heritage is expressed instead by Maristella Rocca.

P.F. Not really. What she is saying has a real edge. When Rocca points out that Italians celebrate the human spirit with violence, and when Patriarca says, "My father punched me in the mouth," they draw attention to the negative side of their ethnic tradition. They are just saying it in different ways.

D.M. I agree, but Rocca lets her criticism come out in a humorous way, disguising it. She is saying it in a tongue-and-cheek way.

P.F. What really should come out is the fact that women had more to struggle with. In order to grow fully as human beings they cannot be nostalgic, as Mary di Michele underlines very clearly.

F.S. Let us move on to a different aspect of *Enigmatico:* how male artists go about searching for their identity. The Toronto-born young painter of Sicilian origin Vince Mancuso is given a more prominent role than the other artists. You present him in different settings: at home in Toronto with his parents, at work in his studio, in his ancestors' house in a Sicilian village, eating and discussing with his relatives, meditating on the significance and weight of his original cultural tradition. Why did you decide to deal so precisely with this particular artist?

D.M. Because, at thirty, he is the youngest, the same age as both Patricia and me, so we can connect directly with what he is experiencing. Through him we were able to visualize what the other artists are talking about in terms of going to Italy at one point in their lives and experiencing something so profound as to alter their lives and their work and, thus, becoming a catalyst for their creative process. Vince is undergoing this process.

F.S. In the utilitarian minded, typical Italian Canadian family, wishing to be a painter is almost a sacrilege in the sense that it is going to be very difficult to make a living out of it.

P.F. That is true, but Vince's parents end up accepting his decision.

F.S. When in Sicily and speaking with his relatives, Vince realizes that going back is not a plausible alternative. He is from a poor, working-class family with limited possibilities. Had his parents stayed there, he would have had the same, if not, more problems to become a full-fledged human being. One of his uncles, a shepherd, points out the injustices still present in Sicilian society.

D.M. The reason that we wanted to keep that scene with his uncles was the harshness of it. There is no way he can romanticize his family's past. That is an important counterbalance for us as film-makers; it warned us against nostalgia, sentimentality. This is what most people left and to a degree is still going on today. The Anglo, mainstream funders and broadcasters of *Enigmatico* could not understand that particular scene and suggested several times that we remove it.

P.F. As Vince says later, his trip is an eye opener for him. There are things he can relate to, but also things he cannot accept. We wanted to demystify the idea of finding paradise by going back to one's origins. The implicit message is: it is tough to make it in Canada, but it would have been even tougher to make it in your country of origin. Vince goes back and takes as much as he possibly can from it, but . . .

D.M. . . . when we arrived in his home village at night in a small van, we had to keep going down in a valley. Vince said, "It was as if we were going into the bowels of the earth." That was exactly what we wanted to show: what Vince could take by going back to the bowels of his family's past.

F.S. In the film there are three family gatherings: the one in Sicily, between Vince and his relatives, the one in Toronto with Vince's parents and the one in Montreal with my family the Riel-Salvatore. Explain the way you used the family gatherings in *Enigmatico*.

D.M. The family gatherings are important as mirrors of cultures. A meal is a way of coming together, of sharing. When researching and making the film we were always eating. That is an important streak to be portrayed.

P.F. Another important element is that as an Italian Canadian, one identifies in relation to one's family and community.

D.M. In the family gathering that takes place at Vince's home in Toronto, we get to know his parents who are both blue-collar workers. His mother's first words in English were "Have you got a job for me?" and his father cannot understand his son's artistic vocation. Although they seem to be supportive of Vince's decision to become a painter, they stress that he would have been the best lawyer in town.

P.F. In the segment dealing with your family in Montreal, we wanted to portray that three languages are being spoken with ease. It is an incredible sense of a marriage of cultures. The meal also allowed to show how both you and your sons are in the forefront of cultural warfare, and finally what children of immigrants will be like in the future. Your children are the prototype of what we consider to be an ideal, the way things ought to happen in the third generation. Languages are not a crucial issue for us living in Toronto. We only have one language: English. But for you in Quebec, the rapport with languages is much more complex. We were fascinated to notice that you were able to imprint in your daughter Eleonore's mind the natural desire to speak Italian with her father and French with her mother.

F.S. The family setting was also a pretext to tackle the issue of Quebec's place in Canada. What we say around the table is juxtaposed with Marco Micone's belief in separation and Antonio D'Alfonso explanation of why he had to leave the narrow-mindedness of Quebec's cultural and political ethnocentrism and move to Toronto.

D.M. D'Alfonso and Micone are the two extremes of the spectrum; they will never work it out, whereas in your family we see the creation of a beautiful trading and interrelation of language and culture. What strikes us is how the best of both worlds are coming to the surface around the table in this household.

P.F. People who have seen the film in English Canada speak about the added conflict in Quebec. It is not only being accepted as part of mainstream English Canada. In

Quebec there is an English/French conflict besides the question of acceptance. It is at the root of what it means to belong. Micone and D'Alfonso embody both sides of the debate. It was important for us to show that.

F.S. After the politically oriented discourse about belonging or being one of the two founding nations which is still unresolved but is at the core of Quebec society, *Enigmatico* looks at the conceptual quest of identity and Nino Ricci becomes its spokesman.

P.F. We chose Nino Ricci because of what he has to say. He is looking for ways to exchange with mainstream Canadian culture. For him the underlining of difference leads to self-exclusion and to a cultural dead-end. We agree with him. His winning of the Governor's General Award is evidence that his writing is becoming part of what we understand to be Canadian literature. His statements have clout, because, although nowadays it is trendy to be Italian, he warns against it; a superficial understanding of Italian Canadian culture.

F.S. Voluntary self-exclusion has to be avoided. The risk of compartmentalized ethnicity is real. I agree with Ricci that the true challenge is to become universal. This, however, does not mean accepting and following blindly the prevailing canon and becoming a caricature. Universality does not exclude specificity.

P.F. I agree. That is what David and I tried to do with *Enigmatico*. We wanted to make a film that sounded right both from the inside and the outside of the mainstream and, by means of different points of view, we hope we were able to achieve that.

F.S. That explains, I suppose, the end of the film. The quest for an identity finally at peace with itself and with a clear awareness of being Canadian is put forward both by means of the sculptor's explanation of the reasons why he chose a specific hill for the building of his cathedral and the words of Verdi's aria stressing the finding, with God's help, of a new homeland, bring the spectator back to the starting point of the circle.

D.M. The film reaches its climax with the sculptor dreaming to build his cathedral after seven years of preparatory work. From then each artist is revisited briefly but the last image is the profile of Mary di Michele sitting inside a moving train. Life goes on and the quest is not over yet.

Notes

1 Vangelisti, Guglielmo, *Gli Italiani in Canada,* 2nd ed., Montreal: Madonna Della Difesa, 1956.
2 Robert Harney was born in Salem, Massechusetts in 1939, where his grandfather had immigrated from Italy. He died on August 22, 1989 in Toronto following a heart transplant operation. Harney grew up knowing that he belonged to several cultural traditions: Italian, Irish, Jewish, American. He received his B.A from Harvard University and his Ph.D in Italian History at the University of California at Berkeley. In 1964 he was hired to teach modern Italian history at the University of Toronto. But as the years went by, his research focused on an aspect of Italian history which had remained, until then, almost completely unknown: the history of Italian immigration to Canada. In the mid 1970s he published several articles on the topic including "The Padrone and the Immigrant," "Men Without Women: Italian Migrants in Canada 1885-1930," and "Immigrants: A Portrait of the Urban Experience: 1890-1930" (with Harold Troper), which received the Toronto Book Award for 1975. In 1979, he published the chapter "Italians in Canada" in the volume *The Culture of Italy,* edited by Julius Molinaro and Bernard Chandler. He also contributed to the volumes *Pane e lavoro* (1980), edited by Pozzetta, *Looking into my Sister's Eye,* edited by Burnett (1986), and *Arrangiarsi: The Italian Immigration Experience in Canada* (1989), edited by R. Perrin and F. Sturino (1989). Harney edited several other volumes in collaboration with J.V. Scarpaci including *Little Italies in North America* (1981), *Gathering Places: Peoples and Neighbourhoods of Toronto: 1834-1935* (1985), and *The Italian Immigrant Woman in North America* (with Betty Caroli and Lidio Tomasi, 1978). Robert Harney's masterpiece, from a thematic as well as a methodological point of view, is the volume *Dalla Frontiera alle Little Italies* translated into Italian and published in Rome

in 1986 for which he received the Bressani Award at the first national conference of Italian Canadian writers which took place in Vancouver the same year. Harney was also the director of the program on Ethnic Studies and Immigration at the University of Toronto, academic director of the Multicultural History Society of Ontario, and past president of the Canadian Italian History Society and of the Canadian Ethnic Studies Association. Robert Harney was considered, with R. Vecoli (from the University of Minnesota), H.S. Nelli (University of Kentucky), R. Gambino (University of New York) and R. Juliani (Villanova University) before his untimely death at the age of fifty, one of the most illustrious and respected scholars on Italian immigration.

3   For English Canada see Brown, R. C. and Cook, R. *Canada 1896-1921: A Nation Transformed,* 1974. See also Granatstein, J. L. et al., *Twentieth Century Canada,* 1983. For French Canada see Ramirez, Bruno and Del Balso, Michael, *The Italians of Montreal: From Sojourning to Settlement 1900-1921,*1980; Ramirez, Bruno, *Les Premiers Italiens de Montréal: L'origine de la petite Italie du Québec,* 1984; Taschereau, Sylvie, *Pays et patries: Mariages et lieux d'origine des Italiens de Montréal 1906-1930,* 1987; Perin, Roberto and Sturino, Franc (eds), *Arrangiarsi: The Italian Immigration Experience in Canada,* Montreal: Guernica, 1990.

4   Bruti-Liberati, Luigi, *Il Canada, L'Italia e il Fascismo.* Roma: 1984. See also Salvatore, Filippo, *Fascism and the Italians of Montreal: An Oral History.* Toronto: Guernica, 1998; Idem., *La Fresque de Mussolini.* Montreal: Guernica, 1985.

5   This text first appeared in *Crosiere.* Vol.1, No. 2, 1990, pp. 117-119.

6   On January 11, 1990 Anna Maria Castrilli, then president of the National Congress of Italian Canadians, requested that the Prime Minister of Canada publicly acknowledge that the federal government had erred when, on June 10, 1940, it decreed the arrest and imprisonment in internment camps of about seven hundred Canadian citizens of Italian origin, accused but never convicted of constituting a threat to national security. On November 4, 1990 the request was granted by Prime Minister Brian Mulroney who made the following public statement: "On

behalf of the government and the people of Canada, I offer my apologies, full and complete, to our fellow citizens of Italian origin, who suffered wrongs during the second world war." Prime Minister Mulroney's declaration finally attenuated the shame that was lodged in the collective consciousness of the Italian Canadian community for fifty years. Moreover, the apology eased the psychological pain felt by the hundreds of individuals arrested and their families for being labeled and treated as traitors. It was clear from the start that the arrest of Italian Canadians was a mistake for they never constituted a threat, nor did they ever envisage forming a Fifth Column or commit acts of sabotage and terrorism. Yet it is only with the hindsight of fifty years that the prime minister of Canada acquiesced to the request put to him from the various interested groups. Even so, as Nicholas Zavaglia observes in his film documentary on the subject titled, *Barbed Wire and Mandolins* (NFB, 1997), the apology was not expressed in Parliament, as many would have wanted. For additional information on the subject see Salvatore, F. "Una semplice questione di giustizia," in *Il Cittadino canadese,* Jan. 17, 1990, p. 3. Idem. "Perdono sì, giustizia no," ivi, Nov. 7, 1990, pp. 1-3. See also English and French national dailies, Nov. 5 and 6, 1990.

7   Cfr. pp. 1-3.
8   See Mazza, Antonino. trans. *The City without Women.* Toronto: Mosaic Press, 1994.
9   Two short biographical sketches exist on Mario Duliani. The first one is by J. Mingarelli, *Gli Italiani di Montreal: note e profili,* Montreal: Edizioni Ciaca, 1980, p. 183. The second is in Antonino Spada, *The Italians in Canada,* Ottawa, Montreal: Riviera Editions, p. 164.
10 Here is how Duliani remembers the events in 1956. "Too much faith! When I arrived in Montreal in 1936, the war in Ethiopia was in full swing. The Italians I met were furious because no newspaper wrote about the war in Africa without accusing Italy of waging a war of conquest. As if the whole of Africa had not been conquered by others who had waged a war of conquest! The older generation, moreover, still smarted from the humiliation Italy had suffered at the time of Menelick. I had been sent to Montreal by the owner a French Canadian daily, *L'Illustra-*

tion nouvelle, which after the war changed its name to *Montreal Matin*. In this daily I had full freedom to say whatever I wanted . . . , but I needed news because *L'Illustration nouvelle* was not associated with any news agency. Luckily, the daily *Il Progresso italo-americano* arrived from New York, and it was easy for me to plunder the longer telegrams it received from Rome and published in the U.S. It was more than a success, a triumph." In *Il Cittadino canadese,* XLVI No. 36, February 4, 1987, p. 14.

11 From a personal interview conducted in February 1988.

12 Duliani was the author of the following works in French: *La Rolls Royce*, three acts, with Jean Reifrogny, Paris: Théâtre des Mathurins, 1930; *Browning,* three acts, in collaboration with Reifrogny, Paris: Théâtre des Mathurins, 1930; *Le Dernier Déluge,* one act, Paris: Théâtre du Grand Guignol, 1932; *Le Secret D'Yvan Krueger,* Paris: Éditions de la Nouvelle Librairie Française, 1932; *L'Orgie,* three acts, Paris: Théâtre de la Potinière, 1933; *Pierre, Paul et Jacques,* one act, in collaboration with Madame Gastice, Paris: Théâre de la Potinière, 1933; *Mam'zelle Malakoff,* four acts, Paris: Théâtre de la Rennaissance, 1934; *Une peu de cendre sur le tapis,* one act, Au Gala de la Société des Auteurs, Paris: Théâtre des Mathurins, 1934; *Le Règne d'Adrienne,* three acts, in collaboration with Paul Brach, winner of the Prix Brieux of the Académie Française), Paris: Théâtre Daunou, 1935. Duliani is also the author of *Théâtre Pas Mort,* a study of theatre, Paris: Éditions Pax, 1933; *La Fortune vient en parlant,* with an introduction by the renowned French singer Edith Piaf, a treatise on the art of stage acting, Fernand Pilon: Montreal, n.d.; *Deux heures de fou rire,* a collection of short sketches on the social and political reality mostly in Europe during the 1930s, where his antipathy towards Hitler's Nazi regime is strikingly expressed), Montreal: Serge Brousseau, 1944. On the back cover of *Città senza donne,* Duliani informs his readers that he is in the process of completing the following works: *La Tragicomédie de L'Amour* (Contes Gais), *Trois heures de fou rire* (Petites Histoires), *Aventures d'un gourde* (Roman humoristique), *Le Grand Sympathique, Le Retour* (roman). It appears that these last works were never

published. Duliani's manuscripts, if they ever existed, have so far proven impossible to find despite repeated efforts on my part. (F.S.)
13 *Cfr.* Bruti-Liberati, l, *op. cit.* p. 152.
14 *Cfr.* Perin, Roberto. "Conflits d'identité et d'allégeance. La propagande du consulat italien à Montréal dans les années 1930," in *Questions de Culture II,* 1982, pp. 81-102; Bruti-Liberati, Luigi, *op. cit.,* pp. 152-153, 191-192. Antonino Spada accused Duliani of being an informer for OVRA in an interview conducted in June 1988, the words of which are reprinted in my volume, *Le Fascisme et les Italiens à Montréal.* Antonino Spada died in Clearwater, Florida, in October 1990 at the age of ninety.
15 *Cfr.* Jean Beraud, *350 ans de Théâtre au Canada Français,* Montreal: Le Cercle du Livre de France, 1958, Vol. I pp. 214-215, 225, 229, 235, 278-279, 283.
16 Rimanelli Giose, *Biglietto di terza,* Turin: Einaudi, 1959, pp. 219-221.
17 Corsi, Pietro, in *Molise Oggi,* XVII, n. 18 pp. 26-27.
18 Ibid p. 238.
19 Rimanelli, Giose, *Moliseide,* New York: Peter Lang, 1992, Preface. p. XVIII.
20 Rimanelli, Giose, "La narrativa di Pietro Corsi," in *Misure critiche,* Conti: Napoli, 1976-77.
21 *Ibid.*
22 Kroetsch, Robert, "A Conversation with Margaret Lawrence," in *Creation.* Toronto, 1970, p. 63.
23 It should be mentioned that the scholarly journal *Canadian Literature* devoted an entire issue, No. 106, in the fall 1985, entitled *Italian Canadian Connections,* to the work of Canadian writers of Italian origin.
24 See Salvatore, Filippo, "The Italian Writers of Quebec: Language, Culture, and Politics," in *Contrasts: Comparative Essays in Italian-Canadian Writing,* Joseph Pivato, ed., Montreal: Guernica, 1985, pp. 189-206.
25 Pivato, *op. cit.,* pp. 153-154
26 See: Pivato, *op. cit.* See also Padolsky, Enoch, "The Place of Italian-Canadian Writing." in *Journal of Canadian Studies,* vol. 21 - 4, Winter 1986-87, pp. 138-152, especially pp. 147-150.

27 Caccia, Fulvio, and D'Alfonso, Antonio, eds., *Quêtes: Textes d'auteurs italo-québécois,* Montreal: Guernica, 1983, p. 201.
28 D'Alfonso, Antonio. *L'Autre Rivage.* Montreal: Vlb éditeur, 1987, p. 108. English versions from *The Other Shore,* Montreal: Guernica, 1986, 1988. Otherwise, unpublished English translations of French originals.
29 *Aknos,* Toronto: Guernica, 1994, p. 191. The English texts are taken from *Aknos and Other Poems,* translated by Daniel Sloate, Toronto: Guernica, 1998.
30 Giroux, Robert, "Mythic Temptation," in *Ellipse* 54, 1995, p.12-13.
31 *Ibid.,* p.13.
32 Caccia, *op. cit.,* p. 193.
33 Caccia, *Ibid.*
34 Minni, Costantino Dino, *Contrasts,* Joseph Pivato, ed., Montreal: Guernica, 1985, p.65.
35 *Ibid.,* p. 71.
36 *Ibid.,* p. 71.
37 *Ibid.,* p. 74.
38 "La Parole immigrée: Interview with Marco Micone," in *Sous le signe du phénix,* Fulvio Caccia, Montreal: Guernica , 1985, pp. 253-272. N.B. p. 263.
39 "La Tristesse et l'Éclat," interview with Mary Melfi, in *Sous le signe du phénix, op. cit.,* pp. 181-198.
40 Esposito, Pino. "Life after Sainthood," in *Eyetalian,* Fall 1993 p. 20.
41 *Ibid.,* p 21.
42 *Ibid.,* p. 20.
43 *Ibid.,* p. 22.
44 Ricci, Nino, *Lives of the Saints,* Dunvegan: Cormorant Books, 1990. p. 7.
45 From *Paul Tana,* written with Anna Gural, Montréal, Balzac: 1997.
46 This interview with Patricia Fogliato and David Mortin first appeared in *Il Cittadino canadese.*

About the Author

Filippo Salvatore was born in the town of Guglionesi, Italy. He has been living in Canada since 1964. His first work entitled *Tufo e gramigna,* about a young man's immigrant experiences, was published in Montreal in 1977. It was republished as a bilingual Italian and English edition as *Suns of Darkness,* in 1980, by Guernica Editions (translated by the author).

Filippo Salvatore's penchant is for the classical style which rediscovers the value of the oral tradition in poetry in the epic manner of Homer and Dante. His favorite subjects are the nearly-extinct peasant way of life, and the contrast between Mediterranean sensitivity and Nordic reserve as experienced in his adopted country, Canada. Using his own immigrant experience as reference for his psychological, existential, sociological, and political analysis of the Old World juxtaposed against the New, he sees himself as the "peasant-poet" who feels the urge to speak for the millions of North American immigrants who were never allowed to speak out. The issue of identity is ever present in Salvatore. He is also a regular contributor to the Italian-language Montreal weekly *Il Cittadino canadese* on topics ranging from Italian Canadian culture to the current Canadian constitutional debate.

By the Same Author

Tufo e gramigna (1977)

Suns of Darkness (1980)

La Fresque de Mussolini (1985, 1991)

Antichi e Moderni in Italia nel Seicento (1987)

Tra Molise e Canada (1994)

Le Fascisme et les Italiens à Montréal (1995)

Scienza ed umanità (1996)

Fascism and the Italians of Montreal (1998)